Good Vibes for
Between the Moon and th

"Imagine you went to just about every beach in every country in the world and made a photograph album out of all the great waves you caught (and some you didn't) — and of all the people you met out the back, or on the road. Then, you turned it all into words. But now you don't have to — Sebastian Kevany has done it for you. A sun-drenched, blue-tinted collage of surfing snapshots."

Andy Martin, author of *Walking on Water* and *Surf, Sweat and Tears: The Epic Life and Mysterious Death of Edward George William Omar Deerhurst*

"The well-travelled Sebastian Kevany has surfed around the world many times at plenty of well and lesser-known places. He is a very observant man who has enjoyed numerous close interactions with various people and cultures. This memoir is filled with thoughtful insights from his experiences and adventures along the international surfer's trail. Lots to dip into and enjoy for all thinking surfers who like to read."

Wayne Murphy, author of *Kanga – The Trials and Triumphs of Ian Cairns*

"Surfing is about more than riding waves. Sebastian Kevany clearly gets that. Read this book to find out why…"

Scott Laderman, author of *Empire in Waves: A Political History of Surfing*

"Sebastian captures the long-standing spirit of Irish surfing, and updates my own experiences of surfaris, adventure, and fun."

Kevin Cavey, the 'Father of Irish Surfing', former Ireland national team surfer and author of *How Green Was Their Wave: The Dawn of Surfing in Ireland.*

Good Vibes for
Between the Moon and the Fire (continued)

"This book depicts many sublime moments of adventure, exploration and surfing from the intuitive mind of the gifted surf traveller and academic that is Sebastian Kevany. It is a true joy to immerse oneself in the nuances of surf culture and the characters in local and far flung realms via the sage pen of such a vibrant author. With his unique charismatic style of writing, Kevany's memoirs open up the joys and challenges of wave riding to the surfer and non-surfer alike. A true breath of fresh sea air in the ever-evolving culture of surf! Míle buíochas (a thousand thanks)!"

Dr. Eoin McCarthy Deering, adventurer, filmmaker and former Ireland national team surfer

"Bassie captures the thrill of surfing in the Wild West of Ireland — a good bloke, writing about good waves."

Mikee Hamilton, Tow Surf Ireland Pioneer

"Sebastian Kevany is that rare surfer who can put surfing into words with inspirational clarity and deep emotion, and explore the deeper meaning of it all. Between The Moon and the Fire brings the surfer's path to life – for surfers and non-surfers alike – via a man who has spent Autumn nights explaining the fingertip's feeling for texture of the ocean as you surf it to Afrikaans farmers in the Namib desert; taught English Professors about the wonders of getting barrelled; and tasted salt spray in every ocean on earth."

Daniel Beatty, author of *Surfing in South Africa* and former Springbok student surfer.

Between the Moon and the Fire

Life in Surfing Moments

Sebastian 'Bassie' Kevany

Post-production proceeds will be donated to the **Surfrider Foundation** and the **Bureh Beach Surf Club**, Sierra Leone.

Between the Moon and the Fire: Life in Surfing Moments

Copyright © Sebastian Kevany, 2020

The author has asserted his moral rights

First published in Ireland, in 2020

Published by **The Manuscript Publisher**

ISBN: 978-1-911442-32-5

A CIP Catalogue record for this book is available from the National Library

Typesetting, page design and layout, cover design by Oscar Duggan (DocumentsandManuscripts.com)

Cover artwork by Elizabeth Cope

About the Author

Sebastian Kevany has been surfing for more than twenty years in California, Ireland, Hawaii, South Africa, Indonesia, Tanzania, Australia, Portugal and Sierra Leone. He has contributed to *The Surfer's Journal* and *Zig Zag* surfing magazine, and has also published numerous academic articles. He lives in Ireland and the USA.

Other Books by Sebastian Kevany

Barefoot Global Health Diplomacy: Field Experiences in International Relations, Security, and Public Health Epidemics

Fever in the Jungle: Inside the World of an Epidemic Troubleshooter

Contents

Dedication

To Sandy, Shannon, Katie, Maja – and anyone else who was cool enough to wait on the beach.

And to McLainer, Richie, and the K-Bay Hellmen, who started it all.

And to the surfers: OMA; el Senor; the Tinker; the Masochist; Jimmy Snukka; Brucey; Systems; Mikee; Art; Conor; Jan; Reed; Willi; Rama; Christian; Patrick; Matt; James; Dan; Rylee; Sam; Matt; Cavey; el Gordo; the Barrel Searcher; Kev Greeley; Tim; Eoin; the other Eoin; Gibbo; Caffrey; Brandt; JJ; Beno; Dave and Shane Lavell; Daz Ultra; Tyrrel; Pedro; Drinco; Pierre; Gordon Getchell; Rob and Kevin and Chad and Bob and Beeper Dave at Wise; the old school guy at Windansea Surf Shop, San Diego; Tooler — and everyone else in the line-up. See you out the back…

Charitable Contributions

Beyond production costs, proceeds from this book with be donated to the Surfrider Foundation and the Bureh Beach Surf Club, Sierra Leone.

Identification

Unlike in many other memoir-style books, no names have been changed – for the really simple reason that few of the cast went by their names anyway.

A Note on Diversity

Though those surfers I grew up with – usually white, male, and European or American; the proverbial good old boys – are no doubt overrepresented in this book, surfing is a sport for everyone: of every background, gender, physique and ethnicity. This book is thus the product of a time and a place: I hope that future works in this genre will have more opportunities to celebrate the diversity of surf culture.

Cover and Author Portrait Artwork

Elizabeth Cope

Disclaimer

This book in no way encourages surfing at night or in other dangerous places, nor does it advocate the occasionally excessive nocturnal party lifestyle that goes with wave riding. It just tells it like it is.

Foreword by Christian Beamish

Christian is a former editor of both Surfer Magazine and The Surfer's Journal; author of "Voyage of the Cormorant—a Memoir of the Changeable Sea"; and owner/shaper at Surfboards California.

Sebastian Kevany's *Between the Moon and the Fire* keeps an eye seaward, in a surfing life driven by sometimes competing allegiances. The desire to be "on it" when ocean conditions align — versus building and maintaining a profession (not to mention relationships) — makes for a push-me-pull-you existence that Kevany skilfully manages precisely because he is, in his very bones, a surfer.

"Bassie," as his crew know him, is a keen observer not only of the surfing discipline, but of the moment in which he is living. Raised in the world of the "time before" (before, that is, the 21st century and its digitised cacophony), in the Ireland of Killiney in County Dublin, Bassie was imbued with a sense of the wonder of the world. And it is this same wonder, that he stumbles upon in surfing — and that he finds in the wide and varied tapestry of the people he knows — that enlivens his book.

Organised around particular surf sessions across the globe, *Between the Moon and the Fire* moves with vagabond surfers, parties, girlfriends, and Kevany's wry sensibility — always with the suggestion that this surfing business is, itself, old knowledge, wrapped up in that same wonder of the world.

Christian Beamish

November 2020

"Plus ça change, plus c'est la même chose…"

Jean-Baptiste Alphonse Karr, 1849

"The parties and party waves of ninety-seven, ninety-eight? Well, I still remember the crazy disco keg party when the cops shut off our power at four a.m., cleared the room with their d-cell Maglites, and found you and your chick passed out against the graffitied livingroom wall, your arm draped over her shoulder …

… they asked me and Rich, 'So who the hell is this?' and we just casually said, 'Oh yeah, it's cool, he's a surfer,' as if it happened every day, and the cops just paused and frowned and kind of nodded and kept moving on. It was all very James Dean sepia – in the pocket, clean lines, and style is everything …"

Dave "McLain" Smith, 2020

"Yeooooooooooooooooowwwwwwww!"

The Tinker, circa Y2K

Prologue

Nausea at Pacific Beach
San Diego, California
August 1996

The sun seared down; my red board shorts stood out vividly against the sand as I lay gasping beside my board on San Diego's surreal Pacific Beach. All around me, ironically, everything was mellow and playful. It looked like a parallel universe as I sat there, solo and shattered: girls in bikinis, families, children. Warmth and sun and the smell of sunblock; the white noise of the surf, the bubble of music and conversation. But in the dark side of the surf bubble I had entered, there was only desolation.

It had been my first real session, in real surf, on a real crowded day in San Diego. I had paddled out at the benignly-named Tourmaline Surf Park, Disneyland on the sand, with some kind of inappropriate reassurance – borne maybe of many lucky prior waves at the edgier but emptier Mission Beach, at off-peak times. Yet it had felt like the most benign possible manifestation of California as I approached the line-up: like a place where everything, and everyone, looked right, and bright, and groovy, and slightly stoned. A place where surfers were the elite and the performers, and I was now part of that show: a place where echoes of Moondoggy, the Bear, Matt Johnson, and other idyllic surf movie icons still hung in the air.

But I had gotten in someone's way, committed the cardinal surfing sin, and been entangled in my leash and caught inside. Had been tuned (surf speak for reprimanded) by a man in a white rash vest: he was slightly overweight and had a spiky haircut and was riding a longboard. Today, he would be dust beneath the chariot wheels of those who had climbed the surfing ladder – but back then he was a god: a more advanced surfer in a place where I was, I had quickly realised, nothing and no one.

He probably wasn't even a bad person, though at that moment he seemed like the devil. I had, for sure, very likely done something wrong – speared him with my board, or dropped in on him, or ruffled the line of swell further up from his take-off. I had no idea, then, that crowds were to be avoided rather than joined: no idea that beneath what looked from the beach like conviviality lay a dark, Darwinian desire to get as many waves as possible to oneself. And no idea, either, that PB wasn't the be-all and end-all: at that moment, it looked like the *ne plus ultra* but, in reality, was several stages below the true surfing holy grail of perfect waves and uncrowded line-ups.

Yet in the tumult of that tuning, everything changed. The buoyant and dreamy confidence I had felt about becoming a surfer, investing what was left of summer restaurant work earnings in an ancient, sun-yellowed board, drained away like water down a plughole – I could almost feel it leaving my body. It was not, it seemed, enough to have friends who surfed, or to have a very cool retro board. Not enough to be fit and young and a good swimmer; not enough just to be feeling groovy under the Californian sun. Surfing would, I realised, demand more than that; many would fall at this hurdle.

How strange – that the ostensibly ultra-simple act of riding a wave – of positioning and paddling for a line of swell lying on a surfboard; of feeling the thrust and propulsion from a line of swell generated from weather far away; of standing and riding natural energy in frictionless glide to the beach – should become so complex, intricate, distressing.

And so I went in and sat on the beach, separated from the friends I had paddled out with, lost in a sea of people. Surrounded, but alone; living out a different reality to the carefree frolics of the beach; the juxtaposition of crushing disappointment and resentment with the sunlit laughter was, in itself, almost laughable.

In a Jonny Utah way, my predicament was compounded by my age: as distressed as a child of five, I was nineteen – an old, old boy to start surfing. Fifteen, sixteen, even seventeen – sure, no problem: bodies are still developing; there is time for muscles to become hard-wired to the demands of oceanic acrobatics. But *nineteen*? Most top surfers had turned professional by then.

Eventually, deep in gloom, I was located. By that time, I had had another brush with the white rash guard – had mumbled a hurt apology to him as he strode past; he accepted, even though still resentful at whatever crime I had unwittingly committed. But, more importantly, by that time I had had a chance to compose myself and decide what to do next.

What a difference that time in limbo made. Found a few minutes earlier, there is the chance I would have given up surfing before it really started. Would have expressed bitter resentment at its lack of regulation, and laws of the jungle; would have been exposed as bereft of the mental or physical makeup to survive. But those few minutes on the beach – still wet and panting under the sun, with the board lying reproachfully beside me – gave me breathing space. By the time the others found me, they could sense, maybe, that things hadn't gone all that well. But there was no talk of giving up.

Introduction

It is barely enough. I have been surfing – the mystic and ultra-cool and slightly absurd art of riding waves standing up on a board – for more than half my life. Yet it will never be the full, surf-from-the-cradle life. That is reserved for those who have been born surfers – or had surfing thrust upon them – rather than having to become. Unlike so many other walks of life, in the closed and curious and protective and intriguing surf universe, even being an accomplished acolyte doesn't always make you the real thing.

Yet I had devoted so much time and effort to surfing – made so many sacrifices in terms of life, location, loves, that I reckoned it had to mean something. Each related course change, in itself, had been necessary and worthwhile – yet some further explanation to myself of why I had to pursue becoming a surfer with such dedication was required. But beyond that, there was all of the memory space it seemed to be taking up.

Recently, a doctor in a pub told me that memory is sometimes a physical event. Certain moments are calcified (or something like that) so that the moment of recall is actually the contents of a protein. I was lost in his terminology, but it made me realise that so many of surfing's moments are lodged permanently, years later. When names and birthdays and girlfriends and other life events have been forgotten (or can only be roused by reminders), there is a file of surfing incidents and accidents that can still be played out, in the mind's eye, at the drop of a hat.

Maybe it makes sense: surfing is all-embracing. The intensity and rarity of its experiences necessarily banishes all other ideas and concerns from the mind – thoughts are, at the very least, turned away from the mundane or repetitive; just getting into the ocean is an immersive event in itself. These brainwashes can be gifts from the gods, but also leave moments that stand out in weeks or months or years of memory that would otherwise blur into each other.

These include wipe-outs, great rides, and encounters with sea creatures; they are also not limited to wave-riding or being in the water, but generally rotate around a single image when the moment of visceral wave-riding experience was at its radical peak. But what were the events that brought one there – why had I paddled out that day; why was that moment so enduring; to what extent did it reflect what was happening in so-called real life?

Of course, the answers are easy. Any moment of drama or excitement or distress is, one hopes, logged in memory for future reference – usually as a warning of what not to do. But to seek out those moments deliberately also takes strong motivations: to make those split seconds happen, that either scar or embellish memory, inexorably requires sets of events and circumstances (often, but not always, unwelcome and distressing) in one's broader life and evolution. Similarly, the logistics of finding and catching waves – the petrol money, time, long drives and manifold other needs – seem, in retrospect, both out of proportion and too easily forgotten.

But why had I – why had anyone – paddled out into the ocean that day? Those reasons are more complex – yet, as I discovered (and which, in turn, informed the structure of this book), they usually fit into a set of quasi-categories: escape from reality or the troubles of dry land, perhaps; a counter-culture move against bourgeois primness, maybe, or the mere forging of a personal identity. Maybe it was the need to evolve as a surfer and reach the next level of accomplishment; maybe camaraderie or machismo, or queasy or sentimental moments of life's crossroads. Maybe it was the search for new sensations, or spirituality, or some sort of relationship with nature: maybe for health, or habit, or addiction, or just the yearning for something – anything – to happen on a grey and rainy day.

Surfing is therefore maybe the product of other causes beyond wave-riding, just as it has deeper effects than surges of excitement. Sometimes, one is driven to it by circumstance, but wave-riding can at other times be the catalyst for greater change; signposts in memory and evolution or indicators of a hopelessly immersive stage of life – be it a relationship or a college degree or a job or a place – with all the trials and tribulations that went with it.

Not all such moments are worthy of deep analysis or review: that would risk repetitiveness, glazed eyes. Other such moments can be summarised in just a few lines in their absurdity or motivation or consequence: only the special few surfing moments have the backstory and domino effects that justify deeper description.

I can see, as a result of these stories, that the time and effort and occasional pain required to pursue a surfing life has been worth it. Without that structure and framework there would no doubt have been other moments in life that would have calcified in memory, representative of key impulses over the years. But surfing seemed to do it all: to capture so many of the decisions and choices and priorities that were implicitly made or determined.

To adapt the cliché that one only starts to live when one starts to surf, one might also say you only start to remember when you begin to ride waves. From grey Irish university days to sunlit years in Australia and Africa; from work missions to Sierra Leone and two-week holidays in the sun to the beach down the road from the family house. From times of solo life or soul-searching or indecision to times of being out of work or underqualified; from times of getting into (or out of) relationships as smoothly as I could: surfing provided not just solace and escape, amusement and excitement, but also a retrospective road map of the ups and downs of life.

Many surfers ride hundreds or thousands of waves in a year; too often the multitude is lodged only in muscle memory and blurred recollection. I, along with many others, have been super-privileged to have had so many magical experiences, even if they leave no physical trace. In contrast, the moments of memory are often the only evidence: hard-earned quasi-war stories, amidst the moments and dates that add up to a surfing life.

Identity

Surf in bones – sunscreen on skin. McLainer prepares to hit the road.

In Ireland, as I grew up, the organised sportsman was a kind of king. In other places there were other gods: different parts of the country paid respects to different deities, elevated mortals for different reasons. In some parts, maybe it was hockey or football or rugby or cricket – but it sure wasn't surfing.

Beneath the organised sportsmen there were demi-gods: those who stood out academically; those who would win scholarships or are going to be doctors or lawyers. Then, maybe, came those who had subculture skills that most never heard about: those who lived for Irish dancing or chess or bridge; those who were into religion or were startlingly good looking or cool or fashionable – those who had an edge of ancient genteel aristocracy in their veins, or who could play guitar, or sing. All of them had it: enough, in terms of identity, to survive.

At the time, I didn't have it: adrift on the sea of Irish university life with an indifference towards scholarship and a tendency to fill up empty hours with fellow revellers in college bars, the vacuum was so vast I still can't quite figure out how I passed the time – beyond elaborate plots to chat up girls. Fortunately, there were still many lesser ways to gain identity in life. Through work or accomplishments, family or travel – through, if desperate, a certain hairstyle or a certain taste in music or beer. Through a preference for hot or cold climates, or the badge of a uniform or a society; through a protestor's banner or a certain type of girlfriend. But surfing was out of the question: the least attainable identity of all.

It is hard to say why any such identities even matter. To many, it is a product of insecurity: your birthright and your background, your environment and your DNA shapes you – that's all there is to it. A *fait accompli:* to try and attain or accumulate other identities through other means is a risky business, suggestive of otherworldliness or arrogance or disdain for the bread and butter of what you are organically entitled to. But what happens to those who still don't fit, even after trying, with assigned identities – those who are still fish out of water?

For them, the search for identity can go on for much longer than the formative years; something that nature and time and fate hasn't yet revealed. To further complicate, one person's ideal identity may change over time or be disdained by others; many may look down on the style of surfing and surfers, long after you have striven to arrive at it. There may even be surfers who don't want to be identified as such (though I have never met one).

But a surfing identity – if that is what you are looking for – is a nightmare to attain. Its get-out-of-jail-free allures are so varied (too much time on the beach? "He's a surfer." Hair too long? "It's OK, relax, he's a surfer.") that maybe it has to be hard to get – otherwise, surely, everyone would want it. Sure, some are born with that way – children of Hawaii or the Gold Coast or Southern California, or those with surfing DNA or bloodlines. For others, status has to be earned painstakingly slowly (even then, it will always be subject to scrutiny and question, like a migrant worker's papers), and often does not even begin to begin to manifest itself until long after one begins catching good waves.

Oh, yes – even that is not always enough. There are many who dabble in surfing and attain identity quickly thanks to time or space, natural ability or circumstance; others who travel and strive and dedicate and yet still never attain that treasured status. Worse, there are so many layers of judgement and snobbery in surfing that identifying oneself as a surfer will, even for great surfers, often be dismissed by the highest élite inner circles – those who have sometimes sacrificed everything else for surfing, and have the necessary wild and searching (and occasionally impoverished) edge to prove it.

Yet for the outsider I once was – and in some ways still might be – there are split second moments in often long and blurred surfing histories when identity can be forged. Moments of actual surfing, by the way – not of hairstyles and parties and beach time; not of sun tans and choosing the right board shorts, though that is all part of the dance, the circus, as well. The moments that stand out in memory for ever, even if they are the events of just a few minutes, or hours, over the course of years.

Starting with nothing but an Irish beachside background and disaffected with sportsman hero worship, university summers in California surf (in between restaurant work, and the dismal return to college afterwards) combined with subsequent travels and misadventures to give me that identity at times when I needed it most. Amidst the dizzying range of choices and destinies that exists for the very young – with all the pitfalls and risks of failure or unfulfillment that each one entails – a surfing identity was my dubious choice.

As with any identity, there were moments of desolation and repellence: moments when hard-won laurels were stripped away; moments when the surfing life and all of the liberalism and lifestyle it entailed could seem cripplingly narrow. Moments when it became meaningless: what good is a surfing identity, in most walks of life – apart from hinting that you are pretty laid-back, most of the time? Yet everyone needs to identify as something, and identities are not tattoos: they can be changed over time. To be a surfer, it was the hardest and best and most unlikely one that I could attain, which only made it more attractive.

First Wave in Ireland
Magheramore, County Wicklow
October 1996

It a totally unwanted way, I realised it was a critical moment. So many elements of the high times of the California summer that had just passed would be, I knew, driven out the door, or into the ground, by the Irish winter. Sun tans would fade and dazzlingly trippy new friendships would be cast to the wind; travel companions would revert to cliques and types amidst the cold and the rain. As we returned to lives of drinking and libraries in wet and grey universities, summers in San Diego would seem like a distant parallel universe, of no currency in the European winter.

So when I was forced to finally discover if a surfing identity would translate into Irish from Californian, I was scared. If it didn't, I feared both that nothing would ever change or evolve, and that the sunlit summer would (in some ways) have been an enjoyable waste of time. I needed it to work: the directionlessness of student life in Ireland felt increasingly heavy; surfing promised an identity, a *raison d'être*.

So, as the sun set and it started to get dark, I felt pressure building. It had been a long drive down to the wave with two Irish surfers, Jimmy Snukka and the Masochist – *noms de guerre*, the latter a reference to *Big Wednesday's* Leroy, rather than any penchant for self-harm – and wasn't the kind of trip that could be done every day. No doubt there would be other opportunities, but maybe not soon enough: one had to make an early mark in front of the other surfers, I reckoned; there was always the looming threat of being judged as not quite cut out for the Irish surfing experience, with all of the driving and bad food and cold and waits that it entailed. If, on top of that, you weren't going to catch waves, it would quickly get tricky for you – as much as for others – to make it all add up.

But by now, they had gone back in to shore. Darker and darker, and still sitting on my board in the Irish Sea: so far, things hadn't worked out; the cold and totally unaccustomed wetsuit (not to mention a lack of booties and gloves, luxuries only later to be granted by the surf gods) and the slight hint of pressure had all led to a series of false starts. I had been riding only very small waves that didn't feel right – that lacked the energy and excitement of California, and that faded out too fast to offer what might be termed a good ride.

Yet even without the sun and the bikinis, surfing still felt worth striving for. As the bluff of the sea cliffs loomed over me and darkened in the night – as the headlights in the small parking lot overlooking the beach came on, as surfers turned up the heating in their cars – I waited. Even without the Cali trappings there was, maybe, a chance that an Irish surfing life would bring other kinds of redemption; that it promised missions to the west coast with cool cats, and an escape from an uber-urban existence: the promise of a connection with nature, and a kind of hippy vibe that was hard to attain in Dublin's dirty old town.

Eventually, as time ran out, the wave came. I looked down after I got to my feet, flying forward on clear water ahead of the curl, and with the moon now in the sky I retained the image. On the seven foot, two inch sun-yellowed and ancient board I had brought back from California, later christened the Cruiser, the water glided by on its rails: in between, my cold bare feet and the white water glimmered in the moonlight. For a few seconds, I couldn't look up: out of all the visions and vistas that could have been imprinted, my feet on a Californian surfboard on an Irish autumn evening in the moonlight won.

Unquestionably, there was the visceral as well. The weightless, floating, gliding feeling was back: a sensation I had only known in America was, it appeared, now available in Ireland as well. Probably always had been, but access had been denied by class and background and upbringing; by a team sports culture, by the cold; by the unavailability of boards, and a thousand other reasons. But now, at home in Ireland, it was here with me.

Stepping off the board into the deep with the sensation of having ridden a genuine Irish wave still processing, I looked up at the cars. The lights of one were flashing, and the horn was beeping – they may even have turned the hazard lights on. That was (I thought) recognition and acceptance, welcome and congratulation – all without the Masochist and Snukka even having to wind down the window.

On the drive home, I thanked them for the good vibes. They looked at each other questioningly, and then back at me. The zip of my wetsuit, they told me, had been down. They had been trying to get my attention from the car park, to tell me to pull it up, so that I didn't accidentally contract hypothermia as the evening wore on. But there was a glimmer in their eye. I still don't know if they saw the wave or not.

Between the Moon and the Fire*
San Diego, California
July 1997

Things were tricky. Just weeks before, I had parted from a girlfriend in Ireland to go back into the wildness and temptation of San Diego for another summer of waiting tables and working in surf shops. An idyllic prospect – yet the melancholy of the separation had deepened under the sun, and everything was off: I was out of synch in timing, style, repartee.

To make matters worse, on the beach at a Tourmaline Beach night bonfire were a big, bellicose crew – not all of whom necessarily always got on perfectly with each other, all of the time. Amidst such challenges, and such local politics, as the revelries escalated, I feared that I had faded into a side act on the summer's stage; just one of those who came along for the ride. Things were so bad that I hadn't even had the stomach for alcohol – a sure sign of distress.

But, that night on the beach, I wasn't about to let schadenfreude get the better of me. *Au contraire:* as the moon rose and the party intensified, with a few others I paddled out into small surf that

---

* Kids, don't try this at home.

was lit by the bonfire, glowed from the recent sunset, was devoid of treacherous currents, and broke benignly and close to shore. No sharks, or other sea creatures – but, even still, probably not safe or advisable, even if there was no danger: probably not the type of thing that one wants to encourage others to do.

But, with the strumming guitars and Bob Marley tracks still audible in the ocean thanks both to proximity and volume, I realised my opportunity. One by one, despite the warm summer San Diego water, the others had gone in: by now, the moon was rising to its full magnificence over the horizon, casting an eerie silver sheen all the way to the beach.

Looking back at shore, I could see the flames of the bonfire rising in the still night rising towards the sky: occasional sparks flared up as someone attempted a fire walk[*] (don't ask). Turning back to sea, I conducted some calculations: what if I rode a wave, or a few waves, while lining myself up between the bonfire in front of me – and the moon behind? Would there be a visual effect?

I didn't know if it would work, or if anyone would notice; even if they did, they might not have particularly cared. Thus, somewhat careless of the consequences but curious of the result, I rode five or six waves, between the moon and the fire, on an eight-foot-six-inch green surfboard called the Hansen. The board was an intimidating object, having been repaired so many times that it occasionally felt like it was made of lead: its ten-inch fin alone looked like a potential lethal weapon. Thus immersed in my relationship with both the Hansen and the Tourmaline waves I eventually paddled in, having pretty quickly forgotten my moonlight agenda.

But instead, something had changed: the trick of the light had worked, apparently, and I had looked good out there. A black silhouette on a long board gliding in to the shore. It had been a surreal and cosmic sight, I was told by those who had, perhaps, over-indulged. Even more bizarrely, there was now a mellower vibe on the beach. Maybe it was just the stage of the night – in the

---

[*] Or this, for that matter....

post-fire-walk soul search, I wondered if the moonlight on the water had itself created some kind of brief spell of reflection on all that gets overlooked amidst the twenty-four seven party.

Who cared, really: if the waves produced a little bit of chill time at the raucous beach party, that was cool with me. McLainer – a local, a few years older, and a more experienced surfer – came up to me and told me I had looked good out there. Something had pivoted: after that, the summer was never the same, and I moved from waiting in the wings to a more prominent role in proceedings.

Today, it seems trivial and distant – but it was, then, unquestionably a decisive moment: a change in direction, even if an infinitesimal and somewhat absurd one. But then I remember how much hinged on such events in those days: how characters would be judged, and image and identity wrought in the public eye of peers for years to come. And remember, also, how long a summer could be in those days if things weren't going right and realise that there had been no choice.

Impossibles
Bali, Indonesia
October 2000

On the back foot in Bingin, I wanted to get away. The wave of the same name in front of the wooden-and-wicker Indonesian beach lodge where I was staying (built, radically, into the cliff above the beach) was a hot house: a tiny and ledgy take-off, and a big crowd, and an over-hollow curl. Three of the things I liked least about surfing, all in one place.

Juni's Warung (as the shack was called in Balinese) was populated by the same surf crew. Every day, the South African and the Aussie with whom I was staying there would come back after having ridden countless waves out front, eyes glazed and blissed out. Only the New Zealander, an older and tall and dark and rangy guy, seemed nonplussed. "Paddle up to Impossibles," he told me. "It's better."

Impossibles – so named because of the way the wave occasionally broke all at once in long sections, making a single ride from start to finish impossible – was down the coast. You could see it from the warung balcony upstairs, but not clearly: the lines of white water broke smoothly along the shore, but that was all one could say with certainty. Occasionally, if you looked closely enough, a small black speck of a surfer would be visible dropping down the face before turning and racing and then kicking out – that was all.

If I were to get anywhere and avoid the looming threat of being a Bingin also-ran, I realised I had to get over there. There was, in a kind of reality TV way, too much attention and analysis going on about waves in the warung anyway: in the same parallel universe fashion, the only thing that mattered in Juni's was how good a surfer you were. When an insufferably cool dreadlocked Aussie or American, I can't remember which, arrived from a high-end wave called G-Land with a very attractive lady telling tales of bouncing off the reef there, he was treated like a god. Fortunately, he had left his camera behind somewhere on his travels and left after only a few days.

And so, one day, I paddled south. Alone at last, I found a section of Impossibles that was unpopulated – the shoreline building-free and lined with swaying palms – and began to surf. There was no doubt that it was not a perfect wave – most times, a section of white water would form ahead, and either take me down with it into the foam or leave me with no option but to dive over the back. Between getting caught inside and dragged by currents, I began to understand how the place had gotten its name.

Yet there, away from the Bingin crowds, I had time and space. Time to repeat the same moves over and over, no pressure, in warm water: time to experiment and take chances and risk blowing the wave because there were no eyes, no queues, no vibes. Time to sit deeper in the curl and watch the lip changing shape around me, even if certain-doom closeouts were inevitable; time, also, to get the occasional good one and fly down the line of the wave. Time to feel, briefly, weightless and frictionless while cruising parallel to shore: time to come off at the end, and float beside my board.

Such denouements were if-a-tree-falls-in-the–woods moments: I had gotten better and better, and maybe it would show some day, but with no one around the elation of good waves and new views and heady advancement was a strange feeling. What would have been grandstand and headline moments had I been with a crew of Irishmen – though they may never have happened, in between repartee and overexcitement and jostling for position – instead went unrecorded, leaving as their only mark a solo hoot and a dizzying surge of adrenaline as I floated on my back, staring at the sky, processing the experience.

Back at the warung, no one seemed to mind what I was processing. But I had the nebulous glow of exhaustion and stoke that gained me some guarded respect, and I drank beers with the South African and the Aussie and the New Zealander that evening. If nothing else, the time and space at Impossibles had chilled me out. Who cared who had seen it, I told myself …

Finning Jonny at Easkey
County Sligo, Ireland
Circa 2001

Amongst surfing's many unwritten rules, there are those that relate to coolness. Much of cool comes – when you play your cards right – without even having to surf; authority and style are linked more to age and weathered features and a slightly beleaguered, yet mellow, countercultural style. That was, at least, the ticket to striking awe into the hearts of younger surfers in the west of Ireland by Mickey and his crew.

A decade or so older, they lived by the surf in converted vans and caravans, living for waves and sporting a new age hippy organic look. They welcomed you based very much on combined surfing capacity, commitment to waves, and deference: any hint of bling was disdained, and every aspect of one's rubric – environmental perspectives, accents, travels, dress, boards, companions, drinking habits – came under their eye.

They were, inherently, cool – they were surfers, after all – but unquestionably held disproportionate power. There was little localism on the Sligo coast in those days, but they could make life good or bad for you in unexpected ways. Effusive welcomes could take the chill out a winter day, and relieve the edginess produced by daunting waves or long drives; tip-offs based on local knowledge of tides and conditions could make the difference between elation and despair. Perhaps most importantly, on crowded days a wink and a nod from one of them would elevate you in the line-up and bestow a rare opportunity to take the waves you wanted.

In order to ingratiate, there were rounds of drinks to be brought, and odd experiences to be endured. Nothing bad ever happened (at least not to me), but it wasn't always quite what I expected. I might sometimes have been as happy with a breakfast roll in Easkey village as with morning rituals of cranberry juice and home-baked brown bread in caravans, but the allure of their support tipped the scales. I knew, as well, that they were at heart being welcoming and – despite their aloofness – most likely wanted company as well.

There were times, unquestionably, when it all became a bit too outré: over the bread and juice, and amidst the smoky mid-morning haze, someone might spontaneously break into a round of sit-ups or pull ups, while explaining their plans for the future of surfing in the west of Ireland. At other times, wafts of aromatic smoke would disorientate and discombobulate the ambience over breakfast – though that was, in its own way, maybe their most genuine gesture of welcome and inclusiveness. Living in a caravan on those barren and windswept slopes, I guessed that any possible variety in perceptions was to be embraced.

So when I finned Johnny at Easkey Right, I had my concerns. Johnny wasn't quite a local but was there all the time and had a giant panel van. He was friendly and easy-going – despite being oversized and with his wavy blond air, buck teeth and glasses, he still had the inevitable hint of cool and distance that comes with experience and status. He was also the confidant of the real local kingpins – and a good surfer, as well.

The waves that day were big and smooth under heavy skies, intermediate to advanced, and I was thrilled just to be there. Perhaps too excited: having taken off on some good ones, I paddled slightly further up the right-hand point to try and extend length of ride, albeit at the risk of a slightly more precarious drop down the face. There, turning to stroke into another one, just a second too late I caught sight Jonny of paddling out in front of me.

So close to the heart of the breaking wave at the top of the point – so near the cold black rocks, and the rolling green hills behind them – there was little choice but to continue the descent. Further down the line of breaking swell there would have been room for manoeuvre, but here there was only one path and – unfortunately for us both – it was the one that Johnny was on. Whether he should have been there was a question never asked of seniors by juniors, and there was also no logic in assigning blame anyway: I had learned long before that in surfing when mistakes happened, youth was at fault.

The split-second moment, despite its brevity, had elements of drama. Jonny, seeing me bearing down on him, registered a look of panic and duck dived into the wave. At the same moment, I rose to my feet and surfed over him: a second later we would have collided; a second earlier and no harm would have been done. Instead, it was something in between: feeling just a sight bump under my fins I knew something had gone wrong, but still travelled down the face of the wave without damage. As it transpired, I had been too deep anyway, and ended up straightening out towards the shore. Though now drifting away, from a safe distance Johnny also appeared unharmed, and we surfed on.

It was only later, disrobing on the roadside, that there was an update on events. Johnny had, it appeared, been finned by me, slicing a nick into his wetsuit, and leaving a red welt somewhere on the back of his pelt. Immediately my spirits fell: it seemed as if hard-earned rapport with the locals was about to dissolve, as I had seen happen to the disgraced before. Approaching cautiously, I looked for clues in his eyes as he starred out to sea while climbing into his jeans. His features held signs of suppressed irritation, though, somehow no (non-physical, at least) harm had been done. Nothing was said: I now apparently fit, just about, into the local mosaic; was accepted, just enough, to be forgiven.

Tuned for Greed at Sunset Cliffs
San Diego, California
December 2002

There are rare occasions, as a surfer, when criticism is the highest form of praise: many is the time I have fumed and cursed hot surfers who get too greedy in the line-up. The difference, this time, was twofold: first, that I was the uber-relaxed one being tuned as to my excess; second that I had no idea that I had been overdoing it. The latter, in particular, seemed a mitigating circumstance that didn't always apply.

Still in San Diego, and by now totally into the SoCal beach groove, I cruised down to Sunset Cliffs at every opportunity. On this occasion, I was with McLain – a both deep and deeply tanned, sardonic and generally topless Canadian surfer, with Ray-Bans permanently clapped to his eyes in his very old and very cool Ford Ranger pickup truck – and his crew: a set of either older and ultra-experienced surfers, or younger athletes. The latter were into it and competent, but maybe would have been equally happy in the gym lifting weights.

The wave was an a-frame, breaking in both directions at one end of the cliffs, and had all the familiar San Diego qualities of sun, smooth oily water, and sandstone rock beneath opulent California houses. The swell was middle to good, the sun was out, and we all paddled out to an uncrowded line-up called Garbage Beach (North Garbage, to be precise, which sounded both slightly ridiculous and quintessentially counter-culture Californian).

There, on an orange board with aboriginal artwork called the Great Pumpkin, I found rhythm and flow. With the water clear and sun shining, the orange would occasionally be visible through the back of the wave, McLain said, as it walled up to curl ahead of me: it was intoxicating, and a lack of exhausting work commitments (or indeed any commitments at all) combined with my age – a rocking twenty-six – resulted in the surfing condition called frothing. I was almost foaming at the mouth at how cool it all was.

Feeling a groovier surfer even during the course of that single session, others began for the first time to take notice. The tattooed and shaven-headed old schooler (who was getting all the waves he wanted) was starting to give me advice – saying I should try to turn at the top of the end of the wave as it finished, instead of dramatic high-flying karate kick airborne exits. Everyone seemed to be enjoying it as much as I was.

Yet back in the car park, there were complaints. I had taken too many waves, one of the gym-surfers opined – calmly, but with a hint of either resentment or envy in his voice. Had been drunk on surfing and youth and life and taken waves that I didn't always have a right to; had feasted with reckless abandon and paddled with over-exuberance to whichever corner of the line-up in which the waves were arriving. Worse, he said, I had been lucky – had been always, that day, in the right place at the right time.

The moment of edginess passed, and people laughed – others told the gym-surfer he was just jealous but didn't argue with him either. But it was a strange and lingering and surprisingly unwelcome sensation: to be the one, for the first time, to arouse envy in strangers: to be for once not the cursing onlooker, but the main event.

The irony was clear, but only to me. Dig just a little bit deeper into the hot surfer's life – a role into which I had briefly been cast – and dark edges and Pandora's boxes appear. The lack of a job or partner or stability; the lack of direction, and the way I was still sleeping on an air mattress on a friend's floor in between restaurant jobs. The way-too-many late nights of drinking and smoking and dancing: all of that, hidden by the good waves I had scored. If they had known the backstory, they probably wouldn't have minded quite so much.

Everything, it seems, has to be set in context. And so – just for a few minutes – I stopped to talk about it. As an ostensibly naïve Irishman, I could have made my escape more simply: briefly apologise, and claim I was overexcited in the California sun. But there was something more fundamental to be explored beyond *faux* diplomacy or brief reconciliation: the unprecedented, bizarre, surprisingly odious thought that somehow there was something in me that was inducing jealousy.

I didn't quite have to tell him the story of my life in the car park – all it took were a few wry glances and oblique references to my real behind-the-scenes condition to quell any unease. So easily, I realised I could have been viewed as an entitled Trustafarian, beaming down from a place where I had everything. But I wasn't: the arriviste image was an identity that – in its absurdity, its vapidity – could, for sure, come in handy from time to time. But it also had its limitations.

Bonassola
Italy
May 2015

In Italy, north of the tourist trail of Cinque Terra, you can swim in deep water at Bonassola Beach. It is a forgotten place, with all attention sucked into the nearby tourist-historical extravaganza. But, when I was there with only a cool lady for company, there was still a bored lifeguard who told me that the next cove over was the best surfing wave in Italy – that there were set-ups I could check on a walk there, even if there was no swell. Boardless and after having swum yet again across the blue-black bay, for the third day in a row, I finally walked down the Mediterranean coast and felt identity returning as I watched tiny ripples peeling in suggestive ways. The waves were a secret message that only I and the lifeguard, being the only apparent surfers, could interpret.

Juni's Warung, Bali; fuel for the flames in San Diego;
clean lines at Easkey right.

Style

Clean lines at Jeffrey's Bay.

Surfing is cool. Such a simple thing to say, but a tricky statement, as academics say, to unpack – even if it is only three words. The problematic one is the latter – cool. To some a clichéd absurdity or a remnant of the sixties, cool is nonetheless timeless. As hard to define as it is to capture – the image of a wave rider standing before waves or sunset, maybe? – cool is also paradoxically and inherently transient. To stay relevant, our approaches and styles have to be constantly recalibrated – yet even then, age and energy and effort eventually lead to occasional lapses: antiquated phraseology, maybe, or out-of-touch standards.

As well as being cool, surfing can also be graceful; can occasionally lend that same grace to one's movements on land. At the risk of sounding dreamy, the fluidity of a wave can, sometimes, transfer on to shore – through the board, up your feet into your body. The coiling and uncoiling and balance – the poise and trim required to do something as unnatural as keeping a surfboard stable on a wave – can occasionally make you less edgy and accident-prone on *terra firma* as well, though this remains scientifically unproven.

Then there is the language. As suspicious of grandiosity and verbosity and formality as a blue–collar-at-heart sport should be, surf speak is deliberately minimalist and esoteric. To follow a conversation between two surfers is to attempt the impossible, so don't try: efforts to decipher will only drive the protagonists further into their provocative linguistic shells. But the pidgin is harmless, and occasionally easy on the ears – sometimes even bordering on the progressive and *avant garde,* as new and *outré* terms slide quietly and gently from the coastal periphery into the mainstream: *lekker,* bru.

Coolness, grace, an element of *cognoscenti*: these are, to some, the elements of style. Every detail and gesture contributes: even the slightest things – which way to drop your board on the sand (depending on whether the sun risks melting your wax); the *whump* as the board hits the beach with just the right amount of disregard to suggest that you both know how fragile and valuable it is, yet aren't so obsessive as to place it on a cushion as you pause for a last stretch and condition-check before paddling out.

At the same moment that your board hits the sand, there is the chance also of a curious glance or two from other beach goers: with wetsuit on, the surfer is no longer a civilian but part of an odd, esoteric and counter-culturally uniformed species. It is, maybe, the relative scarcity of the surfer and surfing culture – rare birds, in most locales – that adds to a self-made subculture fashion of black wetsuits, loose clothes, and flip flops.

Cool, grace, language, ritual, scarcity, fashion: they all combine again as the elements of style. Though probably not everyone's cup of tea – the list of tastes and characters and personalities and preferences that surfing doesn't fit with is endless, from the country set to the upper crust to the right wing – the style is nothing if not distinctive. As a result, sometimes that can be the reason why we go surfing in the first place.

Make no mistake: that is not to say that surfing and surfers are any more or less stylish than those from any other walk of life, or that it is any way acceptable to go surfing because it begets any of these qualities. I, like many, am occasionally repelled by the ubiquitous hoodies, brand names, and material *milieu* of the surfer: like anyone, I crave the black-tie occasions just as much as the down-at-heel, lo-fi casual flip flop life. But if I had to choose between the two, I reckon the latter would win.

Bodysurf at Mission Beach
San Diego, California
July 1996

In the last pre-surfing days, internal forces both pushed and pulled towards the ocean. Something subconscious had to give. Prompts included a deep sense of collegiate drinking unfitness and general seediness: the usual by-products of the first years in an Irish university. The pulls, maybe, were more subtle: at San Diego's Mission Beach, there was a quiet yet irresistible draw into the relative warmth of the Pacific that would never again leave when adjacent to any body of water, hot or cold, salt or fresh.

Thus drawn hopelessly towards surfer style, in between wild nights with comrades-n-arms and restaurant shifts I would swim out into the line-up – staying way, way out of the way – and bodysurf in to the beach. It was the hardest and fastest way to learn ocean lore – riptides and current, undertows and longshore drifts – all under the indifferent eye of the zany boardwalk crew, and to the tune of the metallic crescendos of the nearby roller coaster. Hardly a system to be commended, but there was no time to be lost.

Swiftly after swimming out came body surfing: learning to ride waves in the purest way, which perhaps no amount of later board play could ever match. With nothing on but board shorts, I tried to refine the arm and body positions required for flowing rides from the outside to the beach; there was something in the graduated low tide bottom contours that summer which made it a rolling, ocean-propulsion joyride.

Rather than the top to bottom shore breaks that pound so many aspiring bodysurfers, the accumulated seasonal sand made small waves break for long distances, their even lines of foam perfect for a clean line. One day, on an unusually long ride, the Masochist's girlfriend watched from shore. She was laughing as I emerged on to the sand. "It looked like that was going to go on forever," she said, dreamily, and that was pretty much how it felt.

Van Surfing with Paul
County Sligo, Ireland
Circa 1999

In the most feckless days of them all, every character on a surf trip was both welcomed and deconstructed. With a mate called Les, and a surfer called Paul watching from the shore, I traded waves with Snukka and the Masochist. "It's a Les Paul," said Snukka pointing to shore. Framed against the grey Irish sky – green hills, brown rocks – with hoods up and hands in pockets, amidst somewhat vapid laughter we imagined their staccato conversation: surf spectatorship, particularly with a stranger, is a rough and thankless job.

Later that night, Paul – a telephone engineer and body boarder and only maybe semi-cool, but who had a huge van – offered to drive us from the pub down to Seafields, the local country nightclub where no holds were barred – particularly if you looked the wrong way at a local lass. In the drunken delirium of the back cabin, a spot of van surfing seemed appropriate: with rum and whiskey swilling inside me, OMA and the rest of the entourage were intensely entertained. Using soul arches and switch foot stances, I tried to distribute my weight and maintain my poise as Paul – watching with no doubt mixed emotions from his rear-view mirror – swerved along the county roads.

Yet Paul – who was maybe,, by then thinking we were slightly more troublesome companions than we were worth – had the last laugh: as he hit the brakes outside the nightclub, I careened into his telephone repair equipment, which included shovels and racks of complicate-looking climbing gear. The final act of my van surfing brought the house – or at least the tools – down, but I was fortunately uninjured; anesthetised enough by the whiskey to see it as just the first flourish of the night.

Christian at 3-Ds
County Donegal, Ireland
October 2001

The ocean wasn't delivering – no, no, no, no, no, no. Yet at a painfully-slowly-failing attempt to stage a high-profile surf contest in Ireland – the gods themselves seemed to frown on the bling of its caravan – amidst wave-riding's glitterati lurked a Californian soul man.

Suntanned, white teethed, and in a military jumper, he told me one evening in the beer tent that he was cycling around Ireland on a cross-woven genealogy and surf mission: he was a young author, he said, but was also considering a doctorate in theology despite (perhaps because of) his tastes for wine, women and waves. I offered him our ambulance – an abandoned and converted 1980's Bedford we used as a beachside redoubt – in case he was passing through Easkey, and, along with a gang of Waterford surfers and surfettes, we went through the hazing of a wild and Donegal night and came out the other side.

In his reductionist and slightly functional style – he had once been a construction battalion soldier, hence his attire – Christian also gained acceptance via a brooding dark humour bordering on mild nihilism. Irish surfers took to him, because both of that and a combination of his American naïveté and (less American) appreciation of the complexities of Irish wit; in a welcoming but suspicious society, he seemed so relaxed and low key that it was impossible to think of him ever doing any harm.

He also kept vague karmic accounts: before he left Ireland, he came to stay with my parents in Dublin – but was, at a later date, my and the Masochist's and the Tinker's only-slightly-surprised host in Santa Cruz. More importantly, he was the original owner and shaper, decorator and bestower of the surfcraft referred to in these pages as the Pumpkin.

But it was still strange, just then, in those early days, to see him surf like a king. At a low-key and onshore left-hander breaking into forgotten realms to one side of Bundoran's showcase waves, he paddled out with the host of learners and amateurs that were circling the contest. There, in waves that the hot pro surfer didn't deign to ride, he did incredible things, coiling and uncoiling his gangly and (for wave-riding) over-tall frame and surfing like he himself was half-human, half wave. Flowed with the sections, unleashed power and turns when one least expected it, and stood out a mile on his orange board: everyone watched him rip.

We had a mixed groove; there was something in him a little bit too far-out for my younger self to deal with, and always the (in this case unfounded) suspicion of snake oil that seemed to surround every travelling surfer – particularly the good ones. He was a larger than life character, but his worldliness and experience of war zones and big waves almost made him too rich a dish to digest, at least for an Irish palate accustomed to varying shades of the grey and bland.

Yet, with an extra decade of age under his belt, he offered us a window not just onto what the uncertainties of one's dirty thirties could be like, but also the opportunities that era might bring. He opened up, also, doors to a more real version of California – his descriptions of tensions and freeways and traffic and crowds seemed far from the *beau ideals* of the Golden State viewed through Irish eyes – and prepared me to go west.

Old Boy at Easkey
County Sligo, Ireland
Circa Winter 2001

I had roots and links in Easkey. It is a small town in western Sligo, barren and ancient, whose name, "plentiful of fish", suggests a maritime heritage and economy. My family had once come from nearby, no doubt once fishermen before they all became doctors, and there were Kevanys on the church walls and in the graveyards. Though I felt no special affinity with the cold and rainy and windswept coast beyond the beautiful waves that broke there, my Dad did, and he thus became increasingly interested in coming on surf trips.

In the days when there were fewer and fewer takers for cross-country surf expeditions, not to mention high levels of dependence on the family car to get out west, the partnership made sense. He would swim or walk along the coastal fields while I surfed, chatting to whoever was around. Even the local surfers got into his groove: he had, early on, endeared himself to them by standing on the reef offering whiskey to those emerging from cold winter waters for medicinal purposes, and we went en masse to the local pub in the evenings.

Occasionally, I would even get in to swim with him in the icy depths: much to the amusement of the locals, my jump and swift exit off the end of the harbour wall was likened by the onlooking Mikey to a Tom and Jerry cartoon in which shocked animals spring back out of immersion and run with blurred circling legs for shore, as if walking on water.

All in all, a good enough compromise of universes: drinking and dancing all night on surf trips was bad news anyway, and that was necessarily reined in. Instead we stayed in a relatively upscale bed and breakfast, which – although a little bit precious – was at least a step up from the abandoned and converted ambulance that was usually called home on such missions. Fortunately, also, the swell tended to align when the old boy was around, so there was less of the desperation and over-energised headless chicken wave search that characterised more laddish adventures. The waves at Easkey right, a beautiful right-hander, were in particular often on.

On this day, the right was imperfect but good enough: six-foot waves of clean and clear blue-black water, breaking over the reef. But swell direction wasn't perfect, making the surf more shifty than usual and pushing across rather than over the reef: as a result, the white-water foam stood out starkly from the shore, but in turn made my light blue Rusty six-four stand out nicely by contrast.

For the occasion, to show him what I was made of I caught a lot of waves. The Rusty was perhaps the wrong board for the day, and the swell was breaking far out to sea, but I figured some of my moves would be visible, forming some kind of bizarre quasi-genealogical full circle: ancestors had fished and farmed here; now I was back surfing.

Surely, they had once looked out on the sea, if they had had any imagination, and wondered about the perfectly peeling waves – surely must have seen them as something more than irritating hazards to shipping and sailing? Either way, there could have been little difference between what they had looked at fifty or a hundred or two hundred years ago – there are few topographical changes in this particular part of the Emerald Isle – and what I rode.

All the ancestral dreaminess thus passed through my mind: the sense of ghosts and history, as I laughed at what nineteenth-century Irish fishermen would have thought of their (thus far) *fin de ligne* descendant swooping across waves they had quite possibly hated and resented. At best, I reckoned, they would be looking on with baffled but bemused eyes, seeing their peeling forms finally put to use.

I came in, and the old boy said he had missed all the waves: he did say, though, that the guy on the blue board seemed to be getting a few. I had been half identified, which was sufficient: that wasn't quite the fairy-tale finale but, would have been good enough. But it didn't quite end that way.

The next day, a Monday, we checked it again. The surf was better than the day before, but existential angst had gotten the better of me – pressures to return to work or, attend to other things in life. He left the choice wide open – he wasn't going to be the one to spoil the party, or call time. But my wetsuit was still wet, and the early morning was cold and dark, and the weekend was over. A prisoner still of bourgeois standards and concerns about keeping up with others, despite myself I wasn't yet ready for surfing at odd hours – was, maybe, still too much of a prisoner of the quasi-factory regime that schooling programmes you for to yet be able to figure out the checks and balances that would justify the session.

So there is the lasting image of bigger, but also more perfect, waves being left behind in the early morning darkness. At first it was a silent drive home, but soon I started to try to vocally justify not surfing that day. Thinking he would have approved of my conscientiousness, instead he said he reckoned I should have gotten in. He didn't say much more, but maybe there was an echo too of mortality in his *carpe diem* style: that the memories of Easkey forbears were as indicative of a need to seize the day as much as to worry about the future. The idea that life would work out one way or another, and no one should worry too much: since then, when the waves have been on, I have never driven away.

"It's going to be 'ot"
County Clare, Ireland
December 2003

Moving to South Africa was not as easy as it had seemed. Beyond the logistics and the usual haze that surrounded youthful practicalities, the spectre of the scare stories – the sharks, the crime – would occasionally rear its head. Standing in a shed with a South African surfboard shaper in County Clare just weeks before I was to leave, Ian Johnson of Tequential Surfboards (a local legend; a Saffa; and a good man to know) was sanding a polythene blank. Amidst his craftsmanship, he raised his curly and adamantine head from his work when I told him of my plans. There was little in his words, but sometimes delivery can make all the difference: with wide eyes and gravitas and covered in foam dust, he paused his task. "It's going to be hot, bru."

It came out in in African English as "ot". For no particular reason, it was a quote that delighted others; used as a tag line for years afterwards by local surfers whenever my spell in Cape Town was mentioned. There is little apparent reason why, apart from maybe indicating the insignificance, to the South African, of the issues that plague and terrify its visitors: his only concern was the heat. That was what entertained – that, and perhaps also the quote's reflection of my perhaps slightly over-laissez-faire approach to travel, as I took flight to the other side of the world with just that consultation to prepare.

Encounters with Pierre
Cape Town, South Africa
2004 – 2005

Without anyone to turn to in the early days of living in South Africa, the only choice was to go straight to the top. Outside Kommetjie, between the camels and red dust of the Imhoff Farm, I somehow found my way to the Dream Shop, where Pierre de Villiers lived and worked with his artist wife, Osnat. His was one of the only names I had heard before coming to Cape Town: the hellman who had pioneered a terrifyingly sharky big-wave spot called Dungeons off the coast of Hout Bay; the man who had once been a spear fisherman in the Transkei. Reputedly one of the roughest and toughest surfers in a rough, tough surfing town, Pierre was spoken of in hushed tones as a feral-edged legend in his own lifetime.

The reality matched the myth: even amidst the ultra-high standards of South African machismo, Pierre stood apart. He wasn't disdainful or dismissive of others – ironically, it was the Cape Town surf bourgeois that often dismissed him – but simply operated on a different level. Caring little for modernity, in bare feet he wore Osnat's tie-dyed t-shirts and no-brand shorts while maintaining a quasi-outré self-sufficiency lifestyle and diet.

Learning of my work in public health and epidemics, he told me of his reservations about immunising his children; yet gave the impression – even though he was in no way attempting to – of one so adamantine he would be an Armageddon survivor. One whose system had been so toughened by life and experience that nature, or what was left of it, would embrace and protect him as one of its own: there was, I reckoned as I looked at his wiry frame and bare feet and gap-toothed smile and slightly narrow eyes, no way that he ever watched television.

And so, by an ironic flip, at a time when I found most of the Cape Town surfing massif inaccessible, Pierre – not caring about almost anything or anyone – welcomed me. In his slow precise tones, he talked to me about local waves and shaped me a strange board with an absurdly rounded nose that I had dreamt of: an *avant garde* creation that is, rewardingly, commonplace in these more enlightened times. With the greatest of irony the logo of this most edgy and brittle of hellmen – the picture that I looked down on for two years in South Africa, imprinting it on my mind – is of a star-and-dolphin-strewn butterfly, its wings containing magical lines of swell and breaking waves.

Though we never surfed together – he was perhaps slowing down in his pursuit of waves at that stage, or maybe the stars just never aligned, or perhaps he was always at a big-wave spot – he looked out for me and advised. When I complained that the 1983 Peugeot 504 that I had bought took a vast amount of time to drive to Jeffrey's Bay at its top speed of eighty, Pierre put it all in perspective. "Eighty," he told me, "is a good speed." To Pierre, the high-speed SUV or four-wheel drives that would haunt my rear-view mirror before overtaking me in a cloud of dust meant nothing – would not even arouse reactions of contempt. In his equally ancient Mercedes, he was still too far above them, too strong, and had nothing to prove.

We had more in common than slow cars: between his lo-fi and reductionist existence and my student budget, the board took a long time to appear. "They don't call it the Dream Shop for nothing," some had told me in tones dripping with irony, yet that all seemed to fit with the Morning of the Earth feel of Cape Town's south peninsula – life moved at a different speed. To see Pierre inside his shop drinking an Appletizer soft drink through a straw, legs crossed, and gazing into infinity, was to witness a sole event in itself, which allowed space for nothing else than a greeting and some light conversation.

The board would arrive when it would arrive, and not before – no multi-tasking, which might possibly give me time to chill out myself. Enough time to avoid rushing into the Cape Town surf scene with a splash – to get to grips with Africa, and see beyond surfing, before it took over and narrowed fields of vision. To take, maybe, the surprisingly chilled and cautious approach of the arch hunter, in keeping with both Pierre's speed – and the speed of the Peugeot.

J-Bay
Eastern Cape, South Africa
July 2004 to November 2005

About certain A-list waves such as Jeffrey's Bay, enough has been written. No room, or need, for more paeans in its honour; nothing new to say. No enlightenment in restating the way it is a wave that can briefly make an average surfer above average: the way it sometimes backs off as it breaks, and allows the rider to speed into what looks a very difficult place – down the face, into the pocket, and along the rocky shore – with the greatest of ease.

No need to dwell, either, on the way the wave takes control: the way it propels riders ahead of its power, keeping them in the right place by invisible hands; the way that even the sections that look like they will end the ride turn, instead, into long green faces. Even the way the sunlight, when surfed at certain times of the day, glimmers and radiates off the face of the wave as it curls – lending it an added layer of benign grooviness – has been described in exacting and exhaustive detail.

But there is maybe still a need, even if only barely, to describe its magic. The way J-Bay will accept old boards as well as new; the way it breaks along such a vast length that even relative newcomers to the spot will get what they want – which is often more than they deserve. The way that angular surfers suddenly see the light, as feelings and sensations and muscles align with the wave; the way the wave allows the surfer to relax and cede control. Rather than attempting to dominate, most are so transfixed by its other-worldliness that there is often nothing to do but sit back and enjoy the ride. If surf rhythm can be bestowed at some breaks, at J-Bay the wave rider finds flow: good surfing as a good jazz riff, maybe.

Many such strange things happened to me at J-Bay, and not just in the water: Mikey Meyer, a local shaper, lent me a single fin which

I used on a textured and brightly sunlit day. Before the session, he took us to Derek Hynd's beachside house – an Australian experimentalist turned J-Bay local, who also had a vertical steel slide installed on his second floor. Not wanting to get injured on a toy in a surf Mecca, I passed up his offer of swift descent.

Yet even the wild local characters such as Mikey – and others: one reputedly a former Mossad agent, built like a tank, and who took any wave he wanted – who would provide unlimited stories on their own, are subsumed to the wave at J-Bay. Fights in the line-up come and go – I watched the latter take on a super-fit surfer half his age with his fists and win – as the scent of aloes drifts interminably across the bay. Dolphins frolic and ride the surf; I have looked down the line and seen their grey silhouettes riding the same wave I am. Even on the beach, the coral sand feels clean and therapeutic beneath your feet; at J-Bay, everything natural is supersised and magnified. Yet all that – maybe even all the events of a surfing life – can be subsumed and overshadowed and outclassed by Supertubes.

The *je ne sais quoi* isn't just at sea: On my last session there, a key fin came off my board, washed away, and left me watching in anguish from the beach as the last sets flowed by, the tail end of a fading swell. By chance, a passing American surfer had a spare skeg that fit; between it and his unlikely magnanimity, I was able to paddle back out. The hostel owner, on hearing the story, sucked in his breath and told me it was God's Will.

Like any kind of Mecca, there is a tendency to take note of the strange things that happen there. Like a moving religious statue in Ireland, or the Mystery Spot in Santa Cruz, or Area 52 in the Nevada desert, the accumulation of such stories tends to embellish: to make reputations larger than life. At the same time, if remarkable things do tend to happen in a certain location, they are worth recording. There will never, most likely, be any kind of collective explanation of the things that happen in J-Bay; it is doubtful whether any of them can be described as particularly preternatural. But there is a magic to the place – and it has to be seen, felt, and sensed to be believed.

Bolinas Longboard
California
Circa 2009

Bolinas never failed to disappoint. Up the coast from San Francisco, it was to me just a pseudo-posh Marin town, too often overcrowded with weekend warriors; too frequently hard to find parking amidst the ornate, faux-county shopfront facades. It was meant to be a surf burg, but really wasn't: the waves weren't good enough, and nor (to be totally honest) were the surfers: a place for learners and weekenders, experimenters and occasionals but, not really for those who worshipped at surfing's shrine.

There, however, I was handed a longboard by an old-school surfer and told to relax and try it out. Having earned my stripes at the so-called real waves of San Francisco's Ocean Beach, perhaps I could handle the larger board without fear of degradation: in surfing's youthful hierarchies, longboards are too often the realm of those who don't know enough or care enough and yet still call themselves surfers (there is a lot of snobbery in surfing). It is only over time that acrobatics become distinct from surfing skills.

Either way, this board was different: named after Bob McTavish, a shaper I had met in Australia all those years before (surfing's world is as small as it is snobbish), it felt light and flexible, despite its length. On that Sunday morning in the sun, I tried to surf it without a leash – and without looking foolish: for the first time, I knee-paddled into waves, a dying art, and span my feet and twirled on the board; rode the nose and attempted headstands amidst the lo-fi crowds. Bolinas had delivered: disappointment was driven away by the dividends.

Delayed Reward at Waddell
San Mateo, California
2016

On the yellow six-six at Waddell Beach came moments of pure, selfish showmanship. With the Masochist and his brother – two of the original K-Bay Hellmen, who had taught me everything I knew – I paddled into wave after wave off the side of the Pacific Coast Highway, surfing my best beneath the baking sandstone cliffs.

It was a display of joyous hubris, never to be repeated. Somehow the fates had allowed it: permitted a display of wave-riding and late drops on steep and tricky right-handers that secured me an elevated place in our small surf pantheon. There was no element of hubris or self-justification, any more than a footballer celebrating a goal; I was merely showing off to those who had once seen me with my training wheels on.

Yet there was, maybe, one other element: at a time when they had turned away from surfing – switching to golf, or bike riding – a certain kind of loyalty had been rewarded. Waddell Beach didn't know me, or owe me anything, any more than the Pacific Ocean did. But some nebulous element of recognition from the elements came forth that day – beyond fitness, familiarity, confidence, or the hard work that had gone into finding the right board. The waves came my way; without that, nothing else would have counted.

Pierre; good times at J-Bay; glory days at Supertubes.

Health

Good for the soul: down time at Easkey Left.

In an era in which the developed world is as obsessed with health and well-being as those in more intense need, there are few more attractive avenues than surfing. At once demanding clear heads and responsive muscles, often it appears there is no such thing as an unhealthy surfer. Surfers are thus presented to us as brave, flexible, resourceful, hardy and wily and connected to natural forces.

That, of course, overlooks the elements of both surf addiction and the perennial stereotyped links between a wave-riding lifestyle and parties, late nights, and everything that goes with them. Like any necessity, surfing is double-edged, and has to be handled with care: the line between want and need is a fine one, and too often the allure of oceanic riches and gifts, with all their charm and virility, blinds us to the risks it also brings.

So whether surfing is actually a reflection of ultra-health – beyond advertising images of fresh air, sunlight, saltwater immersion and ocean energy – is a tricky thing to say. For a seemingly reductionist pursuit, wave-riding demands an absurd amount of time in cars, traffic, and parking lots – none of which are renowned for their healing powers.

Then there is the hidden stress: with its unpredictability and intense allure, calibrating lifestyle to catch the right waves (on the right day, at the right time) can give you grey hairs. More broadly, negotiations with the wider world are usually strained to breaking point (ideally just before it); every last second of wave-riding, in far too many cases, has to be milked. Every corner has to be cut – skip the shower or shave, the hairbrush or toothbrush; all sacrificed on the altar of the defining hydro-moment.

And then there are the parties. What else can you do except go with the nocturnal flow when in a warung in Indonesia, or a surf shack in the west of Ireland? In either situation, there are few places to hide – and even if you go to bed it is unlikely you will get any rest. The music will be too loud, the laughter too raucous: better to join than attempt to beat and worry about collateral bodily damage another day.

Yet it is still all worth it: whether you go to bed or not, the health benefits of surfing are so diverse and manifold as to be wildly multi-dimensional. Sun on face, and wind in hair: breathing fresh air, thinking new ideas. Twisting and stretching and strengthening arms and legs; exorcising demons of fear and inadequacy; flushing out hangovers and toxins by throwing yourself over the water's ledge: building lung capacity and sang froid during long spells underwater or, restoring limpid circulation through cold plunges.

Obliterating the damage of heavy drinking with your first duck dive, shedding calories and building healthy appetites: harvesting iodine from seaweed and negative ions from breaking waves: good vibes from dolphins, and salt on your skin. Views of sunsets and horizons and lines of swell that ease and widen eyes and minds; an environmentalist vibe, an attention to diet and even reflections on global ethics – usually, pro-peace, pro-cooperation. Aerobic, anaerobic, cardio, endurance, fresh air: any way you slice it, nine times out of ten the surfer will return to shore healthier than when they left it.

So – like anything, maybe – the health that surfing gives is therefore a zero-sum game. The stakes are merely higher: with the intensity of its recovery power, so too come irresistible temptations that bring you back to square one – double quick. Maybe that is why surfers, despite their often elevated opinions of themselves, are not masters of the universe: despite (or maybe because of) sun tans and strong bodies, they are as totally imperfectly human in their susceptibility to allure, and therefore damage, as anyone else.

Is straining under stress when waves arrive healthy? Are sacrifices, professional or personal, valuable in the realm of well-being? Are missed dates, late arrivals, uncontactability and immersion in a quasi-exclusive milieu necessarily pathways to well-being or enlightenment? Generally not: at the end of the day, surfing is more healthy than unhealthy, but only just. Yet, when feeling off-kilter or grungy, surfing can elevate: when under the gun, surfing can briefly vaporise worries, itself like a drug, railroading the pressures of other walks of life into perspective in a way only natural immersion can do.

That is, maybe, why surfers paddle out when the swell is flat: why they go out on bad days, small days, windy days; why they persevere in conditions that look ugly. There is, invisible to the naked eye, some element of appeal, even of necessity, from a healthy-living perspective: whether it is escape from confined spaces or recovery from debauchery, the surfer's lifespan may have been fractionally extended as a result.

German Girl at Beach Bar
Date Unknown

After a wild night with a German lady in the hotel bar, I strode home in a daze but filled to the brim with the swagger and electric energy of youth. Walking down the beachside drag in the morning light, I saw that the surf was on.

When paddling out later that day, I dropped carelessly and recklessly into waves that towered over my head before kicking out with wild abandon. Even though we were never to see or hear from each other again, each flight down the water and through the air was dedicated to her.

The Old Boy watches Double Wave with el Senor
Killiney Beach, Dublin, Ireland
Circa 1998

For someone who was as visceral as el Senor – the Masochist's older brother, christened via a corruption of senior – he had a remarkable capacity for turning up at soul-bro moments. He would also, for one normally ultra-focused on wealth and status and achievement, lapse into brief spells of reflection before upping his revs again. Thus, on a foray back to the Emerald Isle from what he described to us younger surfers a high-octane London life, we paddled out at Killiney Bay with my Dad looking on.

It was funny, in a way, that he picked up more of a vibe from the old boy watching us surf at K-Bay than I did. In winter, or any time, it is rarely the sort of place for transcendent moments: most waves break unevenly, and there is a survivalism required that leaves little room for cruising beachwards. The spot is normally such a crap shoot, usually so unwelcoming, that to hobble to shore at all is a feat.

Even more unlikely are party waves: moments of looking up and, with thrill or dismay, seeing one of the good old boys dropping into the same line of swell as you. It is a unique dynamic, when the vibe is right: everything in motion – even the observer – and such situations are said to either forge or destroy friendships in surfing lore. (If it is a lady, legend has it that she will be yours by nightfall).

There was no such romance when looking up to see el Senor hurtling towards me, dropping in (or me on him), framed in glittering sunlit water as we cruised in formation to shore. But there was a third actor in the drama: from the winding beach steps, my father had come down to watch, armed with binoculars. Looking up, we could see him waving and jumping, more stoked that we were.

This was rare for a British-style gent, but the exuberance could be excused. A swimmer in the same bay all his life, he had often wished the water was warm enough all year round to allow for winter exploits. He had, also, seen me through some tricky times – deciding what to do and where to go at each next stage of life. To him, here suddenly appeared a solution to everything. Here before his eyes was my new future – and his seal of approval for surfing, and the surfing life: mates in cohesion, with no worries under the winter sun.

Barr na Trá
County Clare, Ireland
March 2001

Sometimes, even the locals lose. At a hidden and protected wave called Barr na Trá ("end of the beach" in Irish) about which we had heard glowing *sotto voce* reports, the Barrel Searcher and Matt and I wound down an Irish country lane to splendid surf: a left-hander, hidden from the view of the main road above, was reeling along from the cliffs in elegant and classy fashion under the morning sun. But it was both a Saturday and Saint Patricks Day, and others were dancing to the same tune as ours.

As we changed into wetsuits at the tight end of the lane – on narrow verges of tufted grass, beside ancient stone walls – the locals shattered the silence with their arrival. At their head was an oversize and frowning red-headed giant, raging at the sight of us:

we were intruders on local territory, he seemed to be saying, as he skidded his wheels and revved the engine of his panel van – the trademark of the authentic Irish surfer – just slightly too close to our bare ankles.

Not knowing how to react, I left choices and decision-making to the others. With a look around and a contemptuous nod, the Barrel Searcher – a veteran comrade-in-arms from the west of Ireland and around the world; one who had forsaken even rugby stardom for surf – continued changing unhurriedly, unhesitatingly. Matt – a travelling antipodean architect who I would later surf with for years in Cape Town – while still unsure of Irish temperaments relative to South African ones, followed suit, though may have emitted an Afrikaans expletive of shock or annoyance beneath his breath.

In an ever-increasing rage at seeing our progress unimpeded by his vibes, the wild one changed and sprinted over the rocks in double quick time. Who knows what his rationale was: perhaps to establish a further degree of territorialism by being first in the line-up, or to warn others of our unwanted arrival.

At a more leisurely pace, we picked our way over the rocks some minutes later. There, amidst the tide pools, lay the local: his ankle badly broken, like the punished villain in a cautionary tale. Yet it was hard to feel anything but sadness and pity and the wish to assist; he had slipped on the rocks in his sprint to the beach, he said, and seemed now on the verge of tears, saying amidst cries of pain – over and over – "Black Paddy's Day." (I was to repeat the phrase when, years later, I broke two ribs on the same crapulous occasion, falling over on to a flowerpot in a late-night, post-party haze.)

It was almost impossible to know what to do. The Barrel Searcher and Matt paused; I hesitated; there was a family tradition in medicine, after all. But, in the same moment, we saw that his henchmen were now arriving to help: there was nothing to do but keep picking our way – extra, extra, carefully – across the reef.

The session itself, despite the good surf, was now unquestionably harder to enjoy: the echo of the confrontation and its sequel replayed in my mind throughout. Having already been prepared for an edgy and localised morning, the low of the accident's aftershock combined with the high of the abrupt defusing of his implicit threat and made me feel seasick: though there were waves close to the base of the cliffs on a beautiful day, it was the tragedy and the confrontation – images of revved engines and a quasi-hated, recently vilified surfer sprawled on the rocks in the sun – that remained in memory.

As with the locals in J-Bay, I wondered about the backstory; tried to see the world through his eyes. If I had been a gigantic and intimidating red-headed local, would I have felt the same way at a group from the other side of the country arriving at a semi-secret wave? Quite possibly: my stance on localism, one of surfing's greatest curses and blessings, had not fully evolved – just then, there seemed only vaguely to be no real right and wrong.

As in J-Bay, who knows what had played out in his life that day, or that year, or years before; who knows what sacrifices he had made that we hadn't; who knew if karma had been suspended, or was in full operation? Yet this had been the product of no misunderstanding or miscommunication: there had been no attempt at subtlety or diplomacy, just out and out Irish ire. There are many ways to skin a cat, and many ways to intimidate: at the end of the beach, he had chosen the bluntest, and paid an instant karma price.

The Heat
County Sligo, Ireland
Circa Winter 2001

The new water centre at Enniscrone hadn't been designed with us in mind. Focused on family entertainment, it boasted water slides, heated kiddy pool, swimming pool and – fascinatingly and rarely for the west of Ireland – a jacuzzi. Yet, with characteristically eccentric and reductionist Irish architecture, all had been located in the same single overarching space. As a result, one mingled in ways that were at once awkward and unprepossessing: a benign form of socialised design chaos, though there was no way of avoiding the feeling that it had not been built to accommodate groups of surfers.

On a flat day at Easkey, OMA and Brucey and I had followed Mikey's firm advice that there was, for us, only one place to go. A hot tub, he recommended, would ease our muscles, and warm us up, after another cold night in the coastal ambulance: the jacuzzi was the first and perhaps the only of its kind in the locale, and had an understandably strong allure for the year-round van dwellers – if not quite so much for visiting bourgeois surfers, of whom I was one.

But there was nothing else to do, and it was cheaper than the more upscale and fashionable Enniscrone Seaweed Baths. Like many other Irish innovations, there was also a strong chance that something would soon go wrong – that it would be shut down, or there would be an accident on the water slide, or the water filtration system would break; those sort of things. With such possibilities in mind we decided to go while the going was good and drove the barren twenty minutes from Easkey to Enniscrone to troop, like a commando unit, into the thick of it.

It is worth remembering at this point that surfers, though often diminutive in stature, are not necessarily small people. Often bulked with muscle from paddling and an outdoor life, the Irish surfer in particular is frequently a formidable, slightly oversized creature. Amidst frolicking and staring families, we trooped towards the jacuzzi. There, non-existent space was kindly made for our beefy entourage between a motley crew of children, blue rinses, and (possibly) a selection of locals.

Shoehorning in, I realised that until that point, I had relied solely on the elasticity of youth to surf. Never before had I understood how congenitally prone we had now become, with age, to the tension and tightness of taut muscles; long road trips and bedding down with groups of surfers in confined spaces had often left me with a feeling of inadequacy as I struggled (and failed) to catch early morning waves. By the evening, for sure, I was surfing with the best of them: it was the cold, stiff, slow and dark dawn patrols,

I reflected in the warm water, that took their toll: that strained capacity, and made me occasionally wonder if I could surf at all.

The jacuzzi that day, is spite of its awkwardness and the slight sense of sanitary repellence, changed all that. Returning to the Easkey left-hander to find small waves curling by the river mouth – dyed an unattractive copper colour by some mineral from the outgoing watershed – we surfed waves that would normally have been too small to catch. Not today: still before noon, my limbs felt free and flexible and rubbery; I sprang to my feet with fluid precision, and even managed to twist and turn up and down the face of the chill surf on the blue and white six-four Rusty – a board I had long felt was too high-performance for my tastes, too much of a Cinderella's slipper.

It had been a heat, Mickey reckoned, who had been watching from the car park: OMA, Brucey, a couple of others, and myself. Even as the unquestionable underdog, I had been pronounced winner of the informal and invisible contest under his eye; the result shocked me as much as others; my place in the pantheon and pecking order had altered, and would be reviewed that evening in the pub.

In the kangaroo court ambience of that dark drinking den, a vast amount of recognition was given to the Rusty – yet, in between, there were heavily-disguised sidelong compliments in my direction. For the first time, I had understood not what my body wanted, but also what it needed. Growing up in Catholic Ireland, that was not something that came easily: to the old-school generation, even a jacuzzi had overtones of sinfulness. Yet, in the pub, still feeling loose-limbed, I felt I could do a cartwheel if required. Another old and harmful belief had been broken down; from then on baths and jacuzzis, stretching and yoga, would be jumped on, or into, at every opportunity.

Wild Times and Redemption at Cregg[*]
County Clare, Ireland
Circa 2002

The surf trips had begun to resemble anarchy. Not necessarily in a malign way, but there was an edge: the unprecedented free spirits that the hazards and the travels and the culture of surfing in Ireland had unleashed were being cross hatched with an age-old culture of revelry that could barely cope with excitement and thrills and adrenaline, on top of everything else.

Rather than being challenged in its role of life force catalyst, party-to-excess patterns seemed to escalate on surf trips – a by-product of fear and youth and freedom. On one mission, Matt had vomited on the dance floor in the Lahinch night club: on the same jaunt, a series of street sumo sessions – in which we would find re-tarred patches of country road, and use them as *ad hoc* nocturnal wrestling rings – was initiated. The culture of the blindside top rope piledriver jump had grown out of it, and at one point – feeling particularly edgy after a wild night, and with some kind of score to be settled with the Barrel Searcher – I started visibly and repeatedly when I mistook a shirt hanging to dry on the bannisters of our rented house for his airborne figure.

The wildness didn't stop there. We bound each other with duct tape as part of routine hazings and there were big hit rugby tackles on the beach, but above all there were the tensions between the reefer and non-reefer smoking contingents. So when OMA and the Masochist produced a tiny amount of contraband in County Clare one evening during an alfresco party, the Barrel Searcher – having (perhaps rightly) had enough of surf trips turning into vague magical mystery tours – threw it into the black night bog.

Thus ensued a frantic and fruitless search for it in the swamp; meanwhile, the Barrel Searcher had moved on, and was now attempting to hotwire a vast piece of farm machinery on the side of the coast road. Barely conscious, he could be seen silhouetted

---

[*] An earlier version of this story appeared in the *Surfer's Journal*, Volume 28, Number 6 (January 2020).

against the stars jamming the controls back and forth, back and forth, in mechanical forcefulness. When that failed, in what could only have been a further anti-drug statement, he unzipped and emptied his bladder from the cabin of the Armageddon machine on to the top of OMA's car.

Even then, there was room for more. When the rain came, the kitchen in the Doolin Hostel was transformed into an *ad hoc* sumo ring; even when corralled indoors, there was space for progress. This time, in a startling innovation, the Barrel Searcher and el Gordo donned swimming goggles and – stripping down to their underwear – squirted washing up liquid across the linoleum floor to lubricate their combat.

Though no angel myself, I hoped that bed would be a refuge from both the ongoing bog drug search and the bout and retreated to the perceived safety of the bottom bunk. But I was wrong: The Barrel Searcher, fresh from his victory in the kitchen, was taking no prisoners. Feeling the bunk being tipped over, I realised I was now trapped in a kind of wooden coffin, with up as the only way out. Before I could escape, there was just time to look up to see his body silhouetted – for the second time that night – against the ceiling, coming in from the top rope.

So when, after all that, the waves got good at Cregg on Sunday evening there seemed to be a chance not so much of surf as of redemption. Amidst the cleanliness and purity of the ocean, a time to silently ask ourselves where the wildness came from – was it a reaction against bourgeois culture, or just boorishness? Were we spoiled and entitled, or merely the latest round of victims in the marketing cycles of the Irish drinking industry; the latest set of deer to be caught in the headlights of a society that had for so long lurched from the wind and cold and rain into the solace of the pub?

Who knew, and – to be totally honest – who cared: all was forgotten when a big, ultra-glassy, and ultra-cold left-hander wrapped into the Lahinch cove on the evening of our last day, glinting and glimmering in the sun. At that age one could still surf after wild excess, and as I dropped down the face the Barrel

Searcher – a little quieter now – was paddling out. It was a vertiginous and tricky wave to surf – not to mention the icy water that required wetsuit and booties, gloves and hood – but there was time to glimpse him paddling over the shoulder of the wave as I wound down the line. After all that had passed between us that weekend, it seemed bizarre that we should now be locked in a moment of affection and respect: as I kicked out with a little *Walk Like an Egyptian* shimmy and paddled back out, he turned to me with a respectful nod. "Nailed it," he said.

It is impossible to say that anyone was redeemed after such a ride. I had played my youthful aces with bells on – had partied way, way too much; had, quite possibly, misspent time and money. Our tails were between our legs yet on the drive home, amidst silences echoing of overtiredness, guilt and the grotesque prospect of office work the next day. But – critically – we had waves to look back on, and that made all the difference.

Cape Saint Martin
West Coast, South Africa
Circa November 2004

Amidst fields of wildflowers – a specialty of the West Coast, or *Weskus*, of South Africa in the antipodean spring – I surfed small left handers at a low-key, quasi-forgotten spot. At Cape Saint Martin, the coast was overwhelmingly verdant in the sunshine; entire fields nearby had turned purple and yellow and blue. The sight was a natural wonder, delighting a girlfriend who had been subjected to too many arid desert odysseys for her more colourful tastes.

Amidst small and weak – but still peeling – left-hand peaks that did little to adrenalise, I surfed my way over the kelp beds as she lay, hippy style, in the flowers staring at the sky. Briefly – too briefly, as it always was in South Africa – everyone and everything chilled out. I had not yet learned to hold and treasure those times – to store them for future reference, amidst the hectic chaos that would inevitably return as their counterpoise. Instead, I merely sensed that benign forces were at play.

With Reed at Ocean Beach
San Francisco, California
January 2007

Driving back to San Francisco from Santa Cruz, late to see our girlfriends, we were surfed out. But youthful fire knows no boundaries: as Reed (an intense and thoughtful east coast surfer who I had met by chance when returning a backpack I had found on the street, and that had been stolen from his car) and I pulled on to Sloat Boulevard in his old-school red Jeep, we caught a glimpse of close-to-perfect dark green autumn waves peeling all the way down the beach.

Fatally, inevitably, we stopped the truck and looked at it. "It is such an addiction," he said, philosophically and maybe somewhat unnecessarily. Like dogs, we guiltily paddled out, and the wave of the moment lined up and cleanly curled over the top of my head as the sound of the lip hitting the water echoed clearly in the still air. Doubly surfed out and almost speechless with guilt, we returned at dark to unhappy welcomes.

Escape from Stanford Parking Lot
California
2017

It hadn't just been the freeways – they were, in all their unpleasantness, by now an accepted part of California life. Gnarly and soulless places, sure, with their constant hint of danger and anonymity – with their slightly martial overtones, and their indifference to society or the environment. Those parts, now, on a good day I had no problem with, even in my increasingly ancient Ford Ranger, I knew how to negotiate and navigate them as best an Irishman in America could.

What had that day tipped the balance away from *joie de vivre*, tilted the needle of temperament towards the red zone, had instead been the parking. Having driven to Stanford University to see if there were any possibilities of working there, I had had the usual series of lukewarm meetings that such meet-and-greets inevitably consist of. Even with an interest in what my protagonists were saying, my mind had been half on the ghastly subterranean parking lot in which my truck was buried and would now have to be extracted from.

The vast amounts of campus construction had meant I had arrived late and had had to drive deeper and deeper into nightmarish and already-full subterranean zones. Behind schedule, all I wanted to do was get out of the meetings, and return home to walk the dog: already, the trade-offs between a happy animal and the possibility of professional advancement had started to stack up in the canine's favour. And so it was with an element of unwanted surprise that, finally escaping and driving past Ocean Beach on my way home, I saw the surf was on.

It wasn't on schedule. Even in this wired and photographed and surveilled day and age, that can happen: on otherwise mixed-up or choppy or unsurfable days, short windows can appear that defy planning and forecasting. On such occasions – and this was one of them, oh yeah it was – a further bonus is usually that few others are out in the water.

Racked with a guilt amplified by the Stanford parking trauma, I postponed the dog walk for an hour and got in. Yet the relief was almost Hollywood: the cool of the water, the warmth of the sun, both in uber contrast to my overheated truck cabin; the deep green of the waves and the bright white of their crests the apogees of the grey freeway asphalt. The oily feeling as I glided down their faces and hooked a couple of long rides in between the vagaries of tide and currents relaxed over-tightened driving muscles: I had gone with dizzying speed from one state of mind, and one way of being, to another.

Looking back out when back on the beach, the waves were already falling apart again. It had been a session that felt like it had been gifted by higher powers; one that restored every equilibrium that had been thrown out of balance by my fruitless trip down the peninsula. When I got home, the dog rolled on its back with pleasure at my return; I joined her on the floor and told her she was too forgiving.

Post-Appendix at Tramore
County Waterford, Ireland
August 2018

I had wanted to leave Ireland, but something was holding me back. It was an indefinable instinct: something, probably, associated with a grotesque and protracted appendix operation of some months before. Everything had ostensibly healed: the doctors had signed off, I could swim and run again. But I hadn't surfed and until I had, it appeared that I wouldn't let myself get on the plane.

Irish summer months are never notable for wave-riding. Characterised by interminably long flat spells, they offer few opportunities to put your body through the acrobatic paces of surfing. And so – expecting little, and still not quite sure what hidden instinct was compelling the trip – the drive to Waterford from my sister's farmhouse in a speedy rental car was ostensibly more of a pleasure cruise than anything else; more a brief escape, and a chance to turn up the radio in true old-school fashion, and hit the road.

On arrival in Tramore, an Irish South Coast surf town, the waves looked unsurfable. Though warm August, a camera would have recorded the scene as the dead of winter as rain drilled down from grey skies, wind tore through sea, and surfers walking by span like anemometers as they held their boards in the gusts. Attempting but failing to rest – to wait it out in the rental's uncomfortable reclining seat – I eventually yielded to the temptation of more driving to check lesser-surfed spots further along the coast.

There, along narrow winding cliffside roads slick with rain, the prospect was no better. The skies barely permitted an exit from the car without soaking through; many more of those kind of hydraulic surf checks would result in aborting the surf itself. Eventually winding up at a half-abandoned harbour that looked like a dream for smugglers, I turned with grim resignation back to Tramore. It was close to six in the evening; darkening; a last throw of the dice.

Upon return, the view was no more encouraging. Conditions, if anything, had deteriorated – but with dusk now looming, there was no choice but to go out. One couldn't have asked for a better day to put an intestinal cavity and peritoneum and rearranged stomach muscles through their paces, I reflected, picking my way across the rocks.

The first wave was a non-event; routine, yet I didn't realise its significance until it had happened; after weeks in hospital and months of convalescence, I was surfing again. No organs or muscles had felt or fallen out of place in springing to my feet, and it was maybe lucky that I hadn't been paying attention: without thinking about it, my pop had felt lithe and easy. The water temperature – as warm as Ireland got – had lent a bath-like ease: after long periods away from surfing, a cold return session can all too easily feel stiff and wooden – mechanical, clumsy, impossibly difficult.

As the evening progressed, the worst the waves got the more I surfed: the darker and windier and rainier it became, the more I and the one or two grommets out (there are no waves that are too bad for the enthusiasm of young shredders) hooted each other. There was, surprisingly and invisibly, a deep skill involved in making crumbling and fast breaking onshore sections that perhaps only an Irish surfer, or a kid, could have negotiated: those exact points of positioning of board, weight, and feet required to make the unsurfable surfable.

The thrill of being back in action, of being fit for combat once more, would last for days. As the surf progressed, inside my body – bizarrely – I felt occasional twinges, but not of pain: more of internal affairs reorganising themselves to surf in the post-appendix era. By not thinking about or recognising it, it was just possible that muscles and cavities and other medical matters resolved themselves in a relaxed way, away from the prying and intense and anxious eye of the consciousness.

With an eye on the church clock on the hill at the end of the beach, I felt, as a further distraction, a brief sentimental connection with Ireland: Under its grey skies, this was the country I had left long before, but that had made me better when needed; a place that, maybe, in some ephemeral way hadn't quite lost its affection for its exiles. As the rain drove across the granite sea walls and the forlorn amusement arcades, there thus arose a bizarre elation that had no right to exist in the grim conditions.

Back on shore, recovery was completed with the sense of having accomplished a kind of surf commando mission: one of those surgical surfs, no pun intended, that you occasionally see. The unknown surfer arrives, often in what looks like an unusually small rented car: checks it, gets in, gets waves. He or she stays out of the way of the locals – but isn't there long enough to offend anyone anyway. Before you know it, with no harm done, they are anonymously slotting the board back into the tilted-back passenger seat; gone into the clouds, or the rain, or the sunset with a wink and a nod.

It was my lucky day, even if luck in the most minimalist and invisible way: I was, for once, that surfer, with all the requisite fitness and finesse, efficiency and detachment. The two bearded tea-drinking watermen – mellowly parked beside me with boards on the roof of their van, as I hastily changed – were in the role I usually played, taking occasional languid or lugubrious looks out at the ocean as night set in. It seemed as if they had, as the song goes, no place to go, no promises to keep – nothing to do but check the grommets and the odd character on the ancient board catch a few. Another wink and a nod – a bare centimetre of a head tilt as I demobbed beside them; a bare lifting of the corners of their mouths in appreciation – was all the recognition needed, the icing on the cake.

Shattered Surfection
Ocean Beach, California
October 2018

There is no perfection in surfing – or as the logo on my board in Australia put it, surfection. Like a chimera or mirage it stays just beyond one's reach, offering only glimpses of its attractions. No perfect surfers, no perfect waves – just, maybe, moments of perfection caught on film; pictures that tell a thousand lies. And so, the flaws of surfing, of surfers, bring the same edges that broader life imperfections bring: just when every variable seems to have lined up, something else goes wrong. There is always, one way or another, a fly in the ointment.

Even so, there are times when it is all too good, too close to perfect, for senses to process – too good even to feel comfortable with. Dropping down a green wave on a sunny day – preferably the first of the session – creates bizarre misfires in primal programming. The wave resembles nothing less, in the glinting sunlight, than some kind of molten liquid emeralds – all the riches of the universe, briefly in your possession. Maybe those are the fleeting moments that are at the heart of deception and illusion of surfing: in the same way as precious stones or metals attract our magpie instincts because of intense visual allure, so too does surfing beget the occasional sense of possessing something that it is impossibly beyond reach.

Unlike diamonds or emeralds, the wave does not last – nor can it be pawned, polished, or resold. Surf is, maybe, the apogee of such material goods – while diamonds are forever, waves are just for a second, yet the feeling of transient possession keeps us coming back for more.

Yet, unlike flawless sapphires or emeralds, something always goes wrong. It is thus, on such supreme occasions, more of a game to see what will misfire. Will the older surfer down the line (who you had written off when paddling out) end up getting all the goods waves – leaving you in the peanut gallery, eating his dust as his rhythm and circuits and cycles run easy rings around yours? Or will you just, *just* miss one – and end up drifting out of position for the rest of the set, the session, the day? Or will the currents and notoriously shifty peaks of Ocean Beach – worth a book in themselves – leave you with an incessant series of mirages, just out of reach; leave you paddling towards imagined peaks which then reappear just where you were before?

After the first wave, that day, a near-three-hour session began in all those ways as I slowly drifted north with the current.

Doubling down the surfection distress, the better the waves, the greater the pressure: the longer you stay into surf, and the colder and stiffer you get, and the more unattainable the magic becomes. Too much sitting, too much staring – posture beginning to cry out from straddling the board for too long – and Murphy's Law results: just as the waves improve yet further, so too can capacity to ride them diminish.

And so on that October day – peak season, in San Francisco – perfect waves were rolling in towards the sand dunes and dog walkers, and everyone was catching them – except me. The sun seared down on glassy water, and each breaking section looked like a work of art carved from glass and light: perfection had never been at once so close at hand and, so far away.

Paddling out earlier, there had already been the feel that it was a bridge too far: my fifth surf in three days, and the swell's spell of peak wave beauty. Something wasn't right: even though the yellow board was going well, even though the crowd was manageable; something had reached its limit. Now, of all times to do so, my body had decided that motivation and strength, flexibility and physical capacity, were no longer quite so close at hand: internally, psychologically, something clicked shut as a result. Yet this was the last chance to get some good ones before the swell faded – couldn't I dig just a little bit deeper, hook one more that would last forever?

Beside me, an ultra-svelte lady surfer dropped in, with feline grace, to wave after wave. All eyes were on her; I took the chance to slide away. On a quiet shoulder, nursing my pride now as much as my body, only one more ride resulted: caught inside after a medium-sized left-hander, shadows already cast over it from the setting sun, I let it wash me in to shore. Maybe the high tide tomorrow would make the waves less ledgy, I told myself, as I tried to walk the fine line of health that bordered too little and too much surfing.

Cape Saint Francis wildflowers; away from the urban sprawl at OB;
clean lines at K-Bay.

Progress

Making the drop at Stilbaai.

In surfing, there is no such thing as progress. Surfers appear to be hatched, born that way: when we behold them on land or in water, there are no certificates or badges or diplomas. In only the rarest cases are there even clubs, that some may choose to represent as a mark of accomplishment or achievement: likewise, only in the most occasional circumstances are there trainers or teachers, rules or recognised bodies. And even when these are in place, there is no correlation between membership and ability; perhaps more importantly, such structures are generally hopelessly unfashionable, and – unless lo-fi and off-the-grid underground operations – treated with a high dose of contempt by the counter-culture surfing massif.

As a result, it is almost impossible to measure progress in the sink or swim world of surfing. Unless you are one of the lucky ones with someone to hold your hand, the most that is offered are occasional brushes with ephemeral senseis or gurus who will most likely just encourage you to continue, to never give up. Almost never is technical advice or recognition offered – or at least wasn't to me. Nor to be fair, did I ever particularly seek it – the whole point of surfing seemed to me to be independence of spirit and style, after all.

Often, then, progress (when it happens) is nothing more than a feeling: nothing more than the sensation of having decoded how to do something on a wave, often without even having realised it; nothing more than a sense of pieces having fallen into place, almost accidentally. Often, also, there isn't even anyone there to witness or certify progress, leaving memory as the only memorial. Worse, progress is too often transient – a turn or a move that worked one day, that felt within your grasp, disappears for unknown reasons the next time it is called upon. The days and even months when surfing progress was visceral, tangible – but then, ephemerally and ethereally, slips away.

Yet, even amidst all of that, progress somehow subtly happens. Even with long gaps between sessions and an understanding of boards and conditions which is evolving – at best – alongside rather than in advance of wave-riding, new tricks are learned. Surfing on white water turns into open green faces, peeling parallel to the shore – which turns into longer and cleaner rides, and wild new sensations. For those who seek them, even greater quantum leaps can then be sought: riding the curl, or explosive turns. Skateboard-style airs, or big waves: just some of the different paths that the advancing surfer can choose to travel down.

Maybe that is why surfers always seem to be born, and not made. Only on the rarest occasions does one witness transitions from stage to stage; only occasionally does a first ride in the curl take place before a prepared and positioned audience. More often, it is with a sense of shock that we see someone riding a wave: with or without knowing their backstory, there is, every time, an element of amazement in seeing someone surf. If they happen to have been an acquaintance who at one stage seemed to have no hope of success – there is an absurdly high burnout rate – witnessing them ride a clean wave is even more incomprehensible. Have they made some kind of secret deal with the surf gods – a Faustian Pact, to advance their skills?

I am as guilty, most likely, of such ostensible anomalies as anyone. Retreating and often by choice surfing solo for long periods, I have on occasion had the pleasure of shocking those who expected little. But progress was so rare, so fickle, that there were many times when I gave up on the idea – times of being prepared to accept that the plateau had been reached. Yet with ongoing refinements to boards and wave choice, not to mention conditions and self-knowledge – a preference for surfing on balmy evenings, rather than stiff-muscled mornings, for example – further progress still seems disconcertingly possible.

Yet progress, thus, is perhaps more darkly tied in with addiction: because of its fickle and coquettish nature, improvement can disappear as quickly and inexplicably as it appears and may pass unnoticed. But even on bad, small, cold, or wind-from-the-wrong-direction days, the potential to reach new levels is there – which is, QED, why we keep going out.

While for most of us the early stages of surfing advancement are without doubt the most exciting and dramatic, the parabola never seems to end. Without doubt, there is probably a point in time where every surfer, no matter how accomplished, starts to regress – though this is often in terms of wave quantity, rather than quality. But, usually, there are opportunities for progress at every age and stage of surfing: whether it is fine-tuning flow and balance and board selection, or subtle shifts in attitude, stance, style. The times when there is that internal click – unseen and unheard to the outside world, and which somehow completes another stage in surfing evolution.

The Curl at Magheramore
County Wicklow, Ireland
Circa 1997

The water was a grey-green, the sky a white cloud from treeline on the shore to horizon out to sea. Almost beyond my control, the fin of my surfboard lodged in the right place at the right time and pivoted the board into the curl of the wave. There before me was its promised and fabled green face – as different from riding the white water as walking is to running free. Suddenly the friction of surfing – and, momentarily, of life itself – disappeared, as I immodestly defied the laws of physics and walked on water.

Rhythm at Tullan
County Donegal, Ireland
Circa 1997

Totally unprepared for life after university, I was drifting. The panic I had seen in the eyes of others hadn't quite set in, but there were frissons and edges. Moments of doubt and darkness – where to from here? If college days had been directionlessness, then the post-graduation world was a wilderness. Too vast and open and barren, actually, to even be called directionless – I didn't even have a title anymore and could no longer shield myself from the demands of the world under the magical aegis of being a student.

Maybe, like so many of those other early-twenties challenges, that was a good thing. Maybe it equipped one to live in the occasional vacuum, and not rely on offices and timetables for sanity. But at the time, all that was unknown – a hazy vision of future-self-sufficiency, that could easily not have happened. As a result, it was time to go surfing.

But chasing and catching waves in Ireland had proven to be hard. The trips were long, and often dominated by wild late nights, with a focus on Guinness and vodka and dance floor moves and not offending the locals. Our surf sessions were thus sporadic.

More than that, the labours of having to drive and change and then drive again – of having to peel off icy wetsuits with clawed hands – take their toll. Learning curves flatten, progress stalls, and a sense of regression creeps in: hadn't I been a better surfer, just months before, in the California sun?

Now, with the wooden weight of primitive wetsuits combined with Cinderella's slipper boards that were too often wrong – not just for the rider, but also the country and conditions (though they had felt fine in board-shorted SoCal) – it was all too easy to lose faith: easier to see surfing as the childish and attention-seeking phase that so many wrote it off as, and go back to watching football in the pub.

So when we pulled up at Tullan – a back beach point on the far side of a Donegal town – it felt like yet another moment of truth. Yet there were for once benign signs: the sun was out, and the hike down the cliffs to jump off at the rocky tip of the point felt less than terrifying. In October, there was still an element of summer in the smell of the grass as we climbed down.

"I should be looking for a job right now," the Masochist said only half-jokingly as he paddled past me with a wild stare upon my arrival. There was no panic in his voice, only a parodied inflection of surf counter culturalism – but the barb was there as well. We were contemporaries, in the same post-university boat; the stakes of the lifestyle trade-offs and choices that had led us there (there were no yuppies in Tullan that day) sometimes felt dizzyingly high. Looking out towards the horizon, I tried to forget: it was too good a day for such trivialities.

The surf at Tullan is usually mellow, and there is a little rip that runs along the base of the cliff to one's left as you look out to sea. The wave is a left – breaking away from the cliffs – but, if you play your cards right, you can paddle across towards the rocks at the end of the ride, and take the conveyer belt channel back out. As a result, on that sunny and increasingly glassy day, there was little to think about, or expend energy on, except catching waves.

On a forgettable six-eight, a fashionable but dysfunctional board, I was wearing a slightly garish red and black wetsuit: despite that, it would be a quantum leap day. For no particular reason, I began to catch a lot of good waves. Because Tullan is relaxed, one could also go a little bigger there – nothing hollow or intense, just a lift and push as the overhead-sized wave peaked and tipped forward, with a light bounce of swell off the cliff to let you down the face smoothly. But the extra size still needed something new – a touch more recklessness, and a willingness to make drops down waves that were significantly bigger than I was.

It became a first experience of surf drunkenness. Just as potent as its alcoholic counterpart (though maybe healthier), the sensation intensified as afternoon wore on into evening. Starting with a little benign dizziness, it later became a question of how close one could go to exhaustion and muscle strain in order to get back outside and snag another one. Amidst uncrowded waves, the day became a feast and a feeding frenzy, which, at its worst, generated an eaten-too-many-cakes feeling of mild nausea. (A surfeit, if you will.) With the sun and the green glassy gleam on the water and the smell of flowers in the air, the elation progressed to a semi-delirious state where cackles of laugher were never far below the surface, and time briefly lost all meaning. For the first time, this was surfing rhythm.

Rhythm is an x-factor, that I have never really heard explained. It is, maybe, a vague by-product of enjoyment and belief – though how such psychological states are connected to being able to be waiting each time in position when the good waves come, tuned into nature itself, is nebulous at best. Maybe if there had been stopwatches or coaches involved, it would be explicable. But rhythm – as I have always since experienced it – is something a little far out: a state of being that is epitomised by picking the right wave of the set, and paddling back out at the end of it with dry hair in a lull, where just a minute before all had been white water.

By the end, I had lost count of how many waves had been surfed. Walking back up to the cars, Mikey gave me a nod. "How many waves did you get out there, mate?" The question meant a lot, though it had perhaps been as much a critique of my count as a compliment. Another bridge had been crossed that day, from one stage to another: a transition, maybe, from Irish surf dilettante to Irish surfer (warm water classifications no longer applied). Life choices had been justified, and his question was the proof; the woes of the real world could wait.

Clean Lines at Easkey Right
County Sligo, Ireland
Circa 1998

The leaden low western Irish grey skies had lifted, reluctantly, to let in some morning light. Below, the right-hand reef break at Easkey looked too small to surf. The paddle out was instead the result of doggedness and a need to clear my head from the raucous small-town pub the night before; the result of guilt and anxiety at a surf trip becoming another night of revelry.

It was worth it: as I sat there, the swell built before my eyes. Not to any epic size, but good enough to entertain Brucey as he watched from the car. Barely believing my luck, I surfed small and clean and peeling grey lines of swell all alone. They were an introduction to surfing at speed, tapering waves, and to sitting in the magical hollow curl of the pocket: even at small size, the waves stood up with elegance and style, and peeled hurriedly across the reef and down the rocky shore.

Soon after, Brucey paddled out. I had, he said, made waves that looked too small to surf seem vaguely appealing. I think it was a compliment.

Forrester's Reef
New South Wales, Australia
Circa July 2000

Seeking that which was beyond our capacity, The Barrel Searcher and I paddled out at Forrie's: a vast peak, which the Australians around us surfed with the ease and familiarity of those raised there, those who checked it every day. Yet there were no dramatic drop-ins for either of us that day, in spite of our joint aspirations to attempt bigger surf. Maybe merely to have been out there was a statement and an education; the power and intimidation of the giant green walls of water, rearing up and breaking on a reef far from shore, felt very much the real thing.

Naked Aggression at Bondi
Sydney, Australia
Circa July 2000

To a young surfer, all locals look the same. There is only over time the capacity to grade the heavy ones into their respective types: those having a bad day; those congenitally possessive; those who are way too far out on the edge. At Bondi, I watched a shaven-headed man covered in tattoos – of which there are many well-balanced and functional and successful examples – surf with brilliance but also a recklessness verging on the destructive.

His capacity was undoubtable, as was his knowledge: on that ultra-crowded and sun-drenched Bondi summer weekend, he took possession of every good wave and every sunlit shorebreak curl that came through – and rightly so. But to watch him weave his board between hapless and helpless tourists, who had no idea of either the magnificence or the danger of the display – as much as the idea that a surfer could quasi-own a stretch of water to such an absurd extent – turned my stomach. With his fins and board far too close to spearing children, lilos and swimming rings, being an accomplished surfer for the first time looked unattractive.

Overreach at Jake's Point
Kalbarri, Western Australia
October 2000

The sun glimmered on blue cold ocean and lit up the reddish cliffs. The place was aptly named – Red Bluff, or Jake's Point, depending (I supposed) on your mood, tastes, or point of view. Whatever it was called, it was the end of the road in Western Australia for us: we had driven too far for too long and this was, we both knew, the furthest north we would go.

With a psychologist girlfriend, who often openly worried about the intricacies of the wave-riding psyche – a few weeks before we had gone into a surf shop in Perth. The owner – a South African called Lal – had welcomed us: hearing of our vague plan to travel around Western Australia, he offered his Land Cruiser truck for use over the coming weeks. I would pay him a little, but there were no questions asked: all he requested was that I didn't take it too far into the desert and get bogged in the sand. With such an offer, there was a jolt of recognition: that one surfer (a surf shop owner, no less) trusted another one enough to lend him his car. Now feeling a full-on member of the subculture – identifiable even without riding a wave while standing in a surf shop – we shook on it.

But with recognition, if that is what it was, came pressure: even if Lal wasn't around, or would never really know how it all went, having a new board and a Land Cruiser and a very small amount of spending money for a month in Western Australia all added up. Everything had been laid out: I was fit, and close to good surf. Now everything else was down to me.

We drove up the Western Australian Coast, north of Perth, and surfed small and obscure waves: Lancelin and Horrocks, and other unmapped spots. There was an element of low-key conquest and tourism to the surfing – almost a collectors' zeal. If the waves lacked quality, and if there was no one else around to paddle out with, then at least I could say that I had surfed there, if anyone was ever interested. (They never have been).

But the pinnacle, the diamond in the coast, was always going to be Jake's. A left point in Kalbarri, an Australian desert mining town, and a long drive from Perth: populations dwindled as we drove north from Geraldton (quiet place, no waves) yet eventually, after only once getting bogged in sand during a beach exploration (sorry, Lal), we made it.

The sun glimmered on the water as we arrived, and a crew of weathered and deeply tanned Australians were surfing the point. It didn't look an easy wave, and I had heard about a local crew who were both devoted to and protective of it. Watching patiently for a little while from the bluff, I eventually prepared to paddle out: after the disorientating and hot and dusty journey, there was no need to rush.

Yet in spite of the sun and blue water and reeling waves, jiving with red desert cliffs to delight the eye, everything was slightly off. In spite of benign appearances, the local pack wouldn't give an inch; in spite of the clear water, the wave broke with deafening violence close to the rocks. Perhaps most importantly, instead of feeling the reckless charging vibe one needed to break into Australian surfing packs, I felt only jostled from the journey, dazed from the sun.

And so, I sat in the ocean and waited. For maybe an hour, as wave after wave broke, and my accomplice got bored of watching and wandered off along the bluff, I alternately sat or lay on my board until I knew, without doubt, it wasn't going to be my day. There was something impregnable about the scenario: even if one part had come right, other elements would have blocked it: even if I had been surfing with groovy and open-armed locals, the bite of the rocks might have been a little too close, the desert just a little too big.

But if nothing else, at least there was the most far-out surfer I had ever met. With long blond hair and moustache, he surfed in front and behind and above and below the curl that day in outrageous ways: despite his advanced age, despite the pounding surf, he would glide past on one leg, switch foot or pirouetting. Singing or whistling or laughing as he flew by, the other surfers seemed to respect but also dislike him. We thus had one thing in common; he was, even if in a different way, also an outsider.

Over the coming days of camping and exploring, he became friendly (though I never caught his name) as I tried again and again to decode the point. But on that first encounter, he paddled past after his twentieth or thirtieth wave and told me that it wasn't going to be my day: that I could wait until the cows came home, but I wouldn't catch a wave that afternoon – not with that crew, on that swell.

Paddling in, despondent and cold, barely having had to move from sitting on my board in the channel, I was greeted by patient, intelligent, but by now querulous questions: she was wondering, quite rightly, about the point of the whole trip. I had publicly overreached myself, I realised: had gone too high and too far too fast; had been propelled by Lal's good vibes and his Land Cruiser and was paying the price. Because if there is one thing waves and surfing itself cannot stand – yet one thing that is constantly offered – it is the reach that exceeds the grasp.

"Do one thing that scares you every day", the blond-haired man told me before we left. I supposed I had done it, but the desert trip was over. Eventually, I had hooked a wave or two at Jake's; we had originally planned to go further north to an even heavier wave, deeper in the desert and called Gnarloo. But for now – at the end point of long flights, long journeys, long searches – limits had been struck, and we drove quietly back to Perth.

Dreamland
Bali, Indonesia
November 2000

In Indonesia, I found the one I had been looking for: not a beau, but a wave; burned out on Impossibles and other lefthanders (waves that broke on my less-preferred backhand, a little bit like in tennis), I walked moodily north, down the beach at low tide, until I reached a bay I didn't yet know was called Dreamland. Warily, I paddled my board over to the edge of the pack of surfers, I was again solo, as I had been for the whole trip: as a result, new breaks now generated only a slight emotional lurch, rather than the extensive soul-searching and local-condition-checking-prevarication that two or more surfers are likely to engage in.

The wait for the wave – the one I had been waiting for – took just a little bit longer. After all, what was an extra hour or two after the days, maybe years, that had, in retrospect, been preparing me for these kind of moments? The line-up was crowded, and I felt only that brittle confidence which comes with solo surf travel: there was no pressure from peers to perform or compete, but no support or group tactics either. No one to shoot the breeze with, which was good and bad: no danger of letting a surf session slip away into an aimless conversation, but no encouraging *sotto voce* exchanges either. There was, at Dreamland, just the wait.

To pass the time, there were small inside waves, but all the while the surf outside impressed more and more. But the water was crowded, and a lot of the Australians seemed to know the place like the back of their hands, so I mainly sat, and watched, and waited. Who knows why – having waited for waves around the world in crowded line-ups – but this was a memorable wait: I floated for long periods on my board, out of the way, watching and daydreaming. Occasionally finding myself thinking bitter thoughts about not getting the waves I wanted, still I sat there: nowhere urgent to go, nothing urgent to do – nothing to do but wait under the Indonesian sun, where time was like rubber.

Beneath its rays, as surfer after surfer got the wave they wanted, it was easy to semi-drift into mental inner space. In such a semi-fugue state, aware enough to stay out of the way of surfers kicking out and dropping in and wiping out and riding tubes, between occasional duck dives and the quirks of current I inadvertently wound up at the top of the line-up – in pole position. Maybe that was the important part – that it wasn't a conscious effort, more just going with the flow. As a result, there were no bad vibes, no edginess, and no stink eyes.

And then the wave came: after only scraps of surf, the best wave of my life thus far. Taking the extra two paddles that Indo surf guides for some reason recommend, the take-off wasn't over-adrenalised – warm water ones rarely are, for those raised in cold climes. Instead, it all happened easily and fluidly until hitting the flats, seeing the lip: right there, without time to think about it, I was for the first time in the Indonesian curl. Not knowing what to do, and somehow getting the angles of descent and traverse right, I registered the Kodak moment of the lip over my head; felt the moment of intensity and excitement of being covered up. Retained, also, the image of the sunlight on the wave and the colour of the water and the bobbing heads in the line-up – even retained a vague idea of what rash guard and board shorts I was wearing: burned on inner retina, it was that kind of moment. But even all of that wasn't the memorable part.

That came after, when a massive, muscled hulk of an Australian surfer with a vastly long beard paddled past after I had finished riding the wave. Sitting there in a semi-daze, and wondering what had really just happened, I was hardly expecting accolades. And at first, it didn't sound like one. "Go in, mate," the grizzled veteran said, eyeballing me. "Go in right now." Unsure of what he meant, and wondering if the moment had been tainted by a territorial trespass, he continued with a slightly manic smile as he stroked past me through the water: "You won't get a better wave all day, mate. Go in now."

Naturally, I didn't. I wanted another one, just as good, but it never came; realising he had meant well, not long afterwards, and after a series of lesser waves, I paddled in. The Aussie had been right – that wave had been enough. By then, the tide was coming in, and the walk back to Juni's Warung in Bingin was no longer an option. Instead, I rode home on the back of an Indonesian dirt bike – surfboard under my arm, along winding tiger trails, and holding on to the back of a bandanna-ed driver with one arm as night set in – all for that one moment.

The Full Stop Rock
Eastern Cape, South Africa
Circa 2005

In the idyllic surfing waters of Seal Point in South Africa is a rock called the Full Stop; there is a pub nearby of the same name. The place is so titled because it boils with circular rippling eddies, just below the surface of the water midway through the breaking wave, causing a full stop to many a ride. If you were in the mood, you can try to surf over or around it.

Beneath the aquamarine, I could see both the light brown boulders beneath and the wave rearing up at the Full Stop. At the last minute I kicked out disinterestedly; said no to running the gauntlet. Whether I would also be able to do so that evening in the Full Stop Pub, a dark and lively beach hang out – was another question.

Stilbaai
Southern Cape, South Africa
Circa July 2005

It was an in-between place, the Cape Town surfers said: no one really went there, especially not the international brigade. Too close to Jeffrey's to avoid its gravitational pull, but too far from Cape Town to justify a day trip. It also just wasn't the kind of wave one travelled for – wasn't either the cinematic double-black diamond or the arena-style viewing magnet. In an ever-uncooperative way, all that only made me want to go there more: it would be a point of distinction, a departure from the surfing status quo; a chance to see another part of South Africa overlooked by most of the rest of the world; and another optimistic attempt to show a girlfriend a good time. The place was called Stilbaai.

From the start, it had the feel of a one-off mission: next time it would undoubtedly be Jeffrey's again, and there were too many other new places to check as well. So it was good when she and I saw, as we peeled off the Garden Route and down one of the Western Cape's countless and nameless capillary roads, that the surf was up: rounding the final bend and bearing down on the set-up, a right-hand wave with vast amounts of white water behind its curl filled the field of vision. There was nowhere else to look, and nothing much else to see: apart from the nearby waves at Jongensfontein and Dolphin Point, Stillbaai was a quiet collection of shops and houses, clustered semi-unaware around a dazzling right-hand point.

The first session was overcast, and a learning experience. The wave had an obscure and esoteric habit of backing off once one had negotiated the drop, yet it still peeled along the round and multi-coloured boulders for a long way. It didn't quite go from hollow to fat in shape as it broke, but somehow changed shape and size and speed. As a result, surfing Stilbaai felt bizarrely prolonged, as one carved and cut back to stay in the pocket; the kind of wave that one had to coax and talk to, almost, to stay in the sweet spot.

We had arrived mid-afternoon, so there was time for a second session in the evening after we had set up the tent. By that stage, the swell had risen even further, and the sun had come out; the water was warm (ever-increasing in temperature as one went east), and darkest blue. Unlike the backlit ultra-green Western Cape waves, the south facing exposures seemed to attain almost a blackness in the evening light.

Beneath her raised eyebrows at a second session, I picked my way across the rocks; there was a constant guttural roar as the swell – still building – hit the boulders. It was the draining noise of water sucking off a shore, but also something else – the deep background drone of ocean white noise, combined with the occasional clunk of big round smooth rocks moving underwater somewhere up the point. Something in the still and vaguely misty air – laced with fizz from the surf hitting the land – captured and held the sound, dampening it.

There were only four or five surfers in the line-up that evening, most of them Afrikaans. Usually, I had found such surfers cool. They were, generally, friendly and modest and not super-hot performers; generally either rural locals or holiday homers; either way, no bad energy or protectiveness. The sun had also started to angle across the water in a particularly dazzling way, coming in from the east side of the point and further (if that was possible) chilling the vibe.

On a Pierre de Villiers seven-two, my board had been made for that day: slightly longer and with a little more floatation that the norm, and the extra length suddenly made getting into waves absurdly easy. Still, there was the usual mix of just missing some, and hooking others. Despite that, as the evening progressed there was also a rotation, a rhythm between the surfers: almost-exact-replica moments, when one surfer would fly past as another paddled back out, each in a repeat or exchange of the same moment minutes before.

Yet there was an edge: the proximity of the break to the top of the point, as the swell built, meant that the take-offs (despite the wave's forgiving and friendly vibe) were getting closer and closer to the white-water oblivion to our right. Occasional glances into the abyss revealed grotesque and unwelcoming looking boils on the surface: if one took off too late, or too close to the rocks, it didn't look a pretty sight – though in the dreamy evening light, no one seemed to mind.

With stakes thus now a little higher, as the evening wore on the swell – by now well overhead, head-and-a-half as surfers say – built again. At some undefinable stage during that pre-twilight, pre-dusk spell – at the right stage, when confidence was up and recklessness was at just the right level – the surf went from good to very, very good. The vibe in the water improved hand in hand with the swell, a fear-and-joy driven *esprit de corps*. But the encouraging hoots of strangers also made one a captive – forcing ever greater lurches of the stomach, as one paddled yet again over the ledge.

The one wave, when it came, was a culmination of all that. But a culmination of the long term, as well, as every wave is: a moment in time when months and years all came into play. It was very big, by my standards, and very, very blue-black. I nearly didn't surf it: swivelling and paddling for it, one or two hoots had already begun, but being hooted into waves is a double-edged sword. The attention can freeze, induce laughter, or distract at exactly the wrong moment; can also invoke unwelcome death-or-glory situations, where there is no other choice but to go.

In that instant, there was no choice – there would be dejection and distress if I didn't try. It wasn't so much the danger – the wave at Stilbaai had a way of letting you in, even if it could still take you and drill you into the rocks if inclined – as the sheer size of the wall of water bearing down on me. With a baleful last glance to my left (now facing towards the shore as I paddled), I could see all kinds of surreal mutations as the swell broke and turned in on itself, just metres away.

Because of this particular wave's shape, it felt vertiginous. There is something, sometimes, in bigger waves that feels totally unnatural: when surf gets to a certain level, instincts reign just as intuition recoils. It is, maybe, a moment of conscious over subconscious – the forced triumph of modern-day glory hunter, overriding years of carefully-developed survival instinct: for one brief moment, 21st century man is reunited again with caveman, biting a thumb at every hard-won evolutionary phase in between.

There was, due to its size, also the disconcerting extra second or two of riding down the face of the wave. This gives slightly lesser surfers a little bit more time to enjoy the ride and is often cited as a reason why those who surf bigger waves are not, on some stylistic level, always very good. (In surfing hierarchies there is always a catch; never a tall poppy.) As the black-blue wall rose up beside me and the die was cast, as I rode down the face with my stomach in my ears, I could feel both pure energy exuding and time passing absurdly slowly. From the channel, the echo of a hoot hung in the air.

The next day the surf was still up, but wind and clouds had come in. The crowd had dispersed, but after the evening before I felt almost a sense of duty to paddle out again solo. The waves ridden the previous day had been so transcendent that there might be a trace of its spark left in other, lesser rides – their contours a reminder of those few seconds of grandeur. But it also looked sharky: to keep my mind off danger, for the first time a parameter of five waves had to be set before coming in. I caught them, but was constantly edgy, almost guilty, and none came close to the night before.

The Moment
Ocean Beach, San Francisco, California
Circa 2017

More and more, I had been surfing solo. With an increasingly bizarre and loose work schedule I could surf when it was empty – on the days when it was perfect, and everyone else was doing something. But it had been a long stylistic learning curve –

sessions had taken on a new shape as one had to set personal boundaries, away from the advice and groupthink of surfing with others, and also in order to avoid either meditative dolphin-watching or gung-ho fitness paddles.

On that day, I parked (as always; surfers are nothing if not creatures of habit) across from the Beach Chalet Restaurant – VFWs to the locals, in recognition of the days when the restaurant was once a Veterans of Foreign Wars memorial. Looking south down the beach from the car park, I could see familiar patterns: the swell was focusing its energy on the middle of the beach, the most exposed part. Down there, as usual, it looked bigger and better – but also more daunting. With the Pacifica mountains in the distance, the peaks rolled and reared and broke for what looked like forever beneath the shimmering sun.

Yet it wasn't a perfect day. There was wind and texture on the water, and a chill in the air. The waves were quite big, but not breaking perfectly; small mountains of white water suggested a lot of duck diving, and my yellow board was getting old. Ironically, it was the type of day when one gravitates towards other surfers – almost always strangers – both as fixed points in the vastness of the ocean and for collective security. But today, apart from occasional distant black dots, no one was around: my aversion to crowds had caught up with me; be careful what you wish for.

But the sun was shining, and I needed the release: in a weathered and increasingly thin black wetsuit reflective of a life that had recently put surfing first, I paddled out and south. If nothing else, I would do a loop and snag a few waves along the way; would chill out, and clear my head, and somehow, incrementally, get closer to surfing better. On such days there was no expectation of quantum leaps forward or heroism: discretion was almost always the better part of valour when alone. After all, what was the point in taking chances when no one was around to watch?

So it came as a surprise not just when the right wave came, but when I went for it. It had needed luck; it was harder to find the right place to be on such days. And added to the constantly shifting peaks was the odd disorientation that comes with having paddled parallel to the shore, from set-up to set-up, without having been able to establish a relationship with any of them. Finally, as I turned around to face the horizon somewhere between Lincoln and Kirkham Streets (the breaks at Ocean Beach also distinguished by alphabetical urban planning), there was a tricky-looking wall of water, but I could see that it was going to let me surf it. Feeling carefree and as if everything were in place – experience and fitness, space and time – I span around and paddled.

It was a right-hander, and there was a long diagonal drop down the face. The yellow board under my feet stood out in technicolour against the white foam inside and the blue sky and the bluer waves; there were flecks and glimmers on the choppy surface as its slightly wind-ruffled texture caught the sun and vibrated through my feet. In the same way, fear mingled with elation, adrenaline, and triumph.

Though not always the best of situations for progression – the solo surfs too often totally forgettable, with no one else around to discuss what had happened and therefore less chance of lodgement in memory – I knew, ending the ride, that a line had been crossed. To have been able to surf a wave well for the sake of riding the wave – to have done it without Kodak courage, or hoots or shouts or any hope of any kind of recognition – was something in itself.

To be able to surf only for the riding of the wave, in other words – and to be able to summon up the spirit and interest when there was no hope of any reward but the moment itself: it had, for once, been enough. If there was a moment when I would have laughed at any one questioning my surf *bona fides* – if there was a second in life where surfing was so deeply established in terms of ability and identity as to be impermeable – then that big and cold and solo and sunny wave was it.

Fear of Regression at Magheramore
Count Wicklow, Ireland
September 2018

In the last throes of another protracted and gnarly degree, and stuck in the onset of Irish autumn, there was no choice but to paddle out at every opportunity. Yet, at such times of highest availability, nature's laws often seem to decree that swell be lowest: the only wave that was breaking that day was at Magheramore – the scene of countless mediocre days, decades before – and it had felt a disproportionate effort to drive the hour down the coast to check it out.

Because of the spot's chequered history in my surfing life, when not abroad for work I had avoided it at all costs. The waves, anyway, were unspectacular: too often failing to deliver the power I both wanted and needed, others – both then and now – somehow seemed to thrive there, making my surfing look even more suspect in comparison.

Yet, for whatever reasons, I drove down. There was simply too little else going on, and even a potentially humiliating session of poor waves would be better than waiting for emails or calls that never arrived. Even with the sun and a lively wind, the mission was edgy: at one point I was sure I had missed a vital turn off on a new road layout, an episode that mocked my efforts at blasé local knowledge after years abroad.

Running late for the tide, at long last I pulled into the side of a country road and made quick calculations. The best move – rather than engaging with the communal semi-nude countercultural thrill of a roadside change – seemed to be to hoist my wetsuit and towel over the side of my board, pocket my wallet and keys (even in rural Wicklow, windows could easily disintegrate), and change on the beach. Such a seemingly trivial decision was to have its consequences.

Gradually, like a receding tide, the walk down the country lane to the waves wove its spell. The grazing cows looking up ruminatively and didn't seem to care if I was reliving the inadequacies and aimlessness of two decades before, when I had last surfed there; they didn't mind about my existential angst or fear of regression. To them, I was at best just another passing surfer – if even that. Yet their indifference and *sang froid* helped: the country soul they seemed to represent slowly began to push back the hectic energy of laptops, motorways and phones.

At the end of the trail – burying my keys and wallet in the sand in a way I hoped wouldn't cause me instantly to lose them – I paddled out. At least there were a few tricks I still knew: how to pick a way along the rocks by the shore to the south end of the cove to avoid the inside white water; which way the current ran along the base of the cliff. But, most importantly, there were waves: at least a vague capacity to forecast conditions here based on a glance at the home beach had not, it seemed, been completely eroded.

Out the back, there were some surfers who I hadn't seen in years, and others I had never seen before. Gradually, in front of both groups, I unexpectedly started getting good waves. I couldn't be sure, however: it is too often hard to tell if one is surfing well, thinks one is surfing well, or is just lucky: often, *joie de vivre* can rekindle just from paddling out. But with the occasional hoot between the circuits from breaking wave to shore to paddle back it felt as if, unexpectedly, this would be my day.

It had never been that way before at Magheramore. There was always someone else: someone better or faster or luckier; someone more in tune, more accomplished. As a result, it took me time to understand I was now the one in the limelight; that a decade of devotion in Cali had its benefits; that I was the one paddling zealously and smoothly for each set. That I was, by some twist of fate, the one in the right place at the right time.

Momentarily trying to pinpoint the pivot when the dejection I had felt earlier that day had morphed unrecognisably into capacity and assurance, ease and invincibility, I couldn't quite put my finger on it. It had been a gradual change, rather than any one moment of culmination or revelation. Only tiredness eventually drove me into the beach, but even the *denouement* was right on as a bearded surfer raised a hand in salute as I cruised by in the last of the glimmering sunlight. Even the weather was cooperating. In the fading but warm sun, I changed on the beach and perched on a rock to watch the others.

But the good vibes didn't end there. A New Zealander and his mate approached me, paying an indirect compliment by examining my ancient Cruiser – the same craft surfed there twenty years before – and telling me that it looked to them as if it had been the right board for the day. It was maybe with that sidelong recognition that all the angst that had dominated the day, week, and month up to that point lifted completely: the combination of good vibes and good waves was too much even for a brooding unease to resist.

I felt, also, fit and efficient: I had surfed many, many waves in the space of an hour, rather than allowing myself to drift into the spaced-out and dreamy surf reflections of yesteryear. But, above all, there had been a failure to regress: no recidivism ; no sign of the timequake to suck me back into the state of mind and surfing ability of twenty years before that I had superstitiously and irrationally feared. Everything had lined up; it was time to go home.

But to what? The recollection of regrets at having left good days of surf in the past, combined with the repellent prospect of returning to a laptop computer, made me pause. There was, for better but probably for worse, no need to be in a rush. The casual repartee with the Kiwi was a reminder to chill out and take the scenic route; it had been a long drive down, so the decision to change back into a wet wetsuit and get back in the water seemed to be a simple one.

It was only when paddling back out that I realised the peril of my situation. Having escaped the shadows of the past with a few laurels, I was now – like a gambler redoubling his bets after a winning hand – risking slipping into them again. All too late, I recognised that I was now tired and cold and increasingly stiff; that the decision to never turn away from good waves would always be rewarding and right in the long term, but that every self-made rule had its exception. That, also, the beach and the waves now had the upper hand again: paddling limply to catch two or three, and the wave-riding nowhere near the level of style and quality that had characterised the hour before. Just in time, I realised that the game was up, and that breaking even would now have to be enough.

The undulation suggests the Full Stop rock lies ahead — Seal Point; a lucky customer amidst the aloes at J-Bay; hoots from the shoulder at Stilbaai.

Escape

Dodging kelp heads at Elands.

Surfing isn't always beautiful or benign or therapeutic. It can take away as much as it gives; can compress as much breathing space as it gives. Can be escapist fantasy, as much as therapy – can take up hours and weeks and months and years of time, while the rest of the world is placed in suspended animation.

For the surfer, this is perhaps connected with images of Ponce de Leon and eternal youth: surfing, if it doesn't help to dodge the bullets of adult responsibility, can at least delay or divert their course. While others are faced by the chronological sequence of events that life demands – its bridges to be crossed, its stages or growth and evolution – surfing can provide a stealthy means of escape when it is all happening too fast.

Yet escapism isn't always malign: In many cases, it can be of the best kind. A chance to totally forget problems for a while, returning to them calmer and clearer and with saltwater dripping from your nose; a chance to leave every trouble and bitter memory back on dry land. But, like any escape, most problems are generally not solved on return – some time out, some fade, but most remain. Yet at least surfing is not drinking or pharmaceuticals or smoking, even though it has been compared to all three: at least with oceanic escapes, the only destruction is to deadlines.

At its peak, such escape creates a state of consciousness in which moody memories melt under hot sun, or distress is dissolved in glimmering water. Usually, though, surfing offers just a little bit of space: time, when faced with seemingly unmakeable decisions and choices, or when manifold pressures grow too high in terms of education, work, relationships, or any other combination of life's challenges. In the water, everything is briefly wiped and forgotten, torn down and reconstructed.

On the flip side, and at its worst, escapism represents equivocation and prevarication: it ignores the needs of others, and dodges work. At such times, it is hard to say if it is good or bad to go surfing. In the refuge from open availability, and therefore scrutiny – like images of a remote country house or a mountain redoubt – in the ocean one is often untouchable, uncontactable.

As with sailing or rock climbing, mediation or yoga, there is (albeit briefly) no way you can be pounced on – no email or text message grenades (let's just hope it wasn't an emergency). Even if these are waiting inexorably upon return to a cell phone or a computer screen, the escape has sometimes worked: contingencies have been worked out, problems have been processed, Plan Bs figured out.

South and North Point
Western Australia
Circa October 2000

For no particular reason, Maja had taken against Mark. In the verdant wine country of Australia's Margaret River, she and I had intended to surf and drink Malbec and travel. But Mark, staying in the same hostel, was in need of a ride: an American and a super-surfer, he was travelling alone while recharging his Indonesian visa, and seemed somewhat adrift. We had met in the hostel bar and again in the bathroom, where he explained his repeated visits there in laddish terms as "breaking the seal".

I was doing, I reckoned in my slightly hippy way, nothing more than what was expected of one surfer from another: helping out, hanging out, driving to waves – though I knew I would never have had either the skills or the confidence or the blithe opportunism to insert myself into other lives in quite his way. (Years later in South Africa, Matt would make sure that if I wanted to get to waves – at least in the early days – then I had to get there myself.)

And so she and he and I drove and surfed together: at main break Margaret's, a daunting big-wave spot, I caught shoulders but was deeply impressed by his deep take-offs. His skill and style were hypnotic: was everything I wanted to be. And so, as the days went by, we ranged to further distant waves, to North Point, a fast and intense right-hander a little way up the coast.

With all the blithe assurance not just of a travelling westerner but also that of an affluent Californian surfer, Mark took off on big and fast waves, and raced down the line. Often too steep and ledgy and powerful for my skills – breaking with too much hollowness and ferocity, the lip detonating as it impacted – I paddled in early on the days when it wasn't going my way.

Mark didn't seem to notice. It wasn't that he was bad, or even dumb; he was accomplished and talented in the water, but maybes just oblivious to the subtleties of life on land. He was undoubtedly a privileged creature from a planet closer to the sun, but also one that had been reared in captivity; his lack of finesse and diplomacy could perhaps be excused only on that basis.

So when I made the switch – amidst my own slight resentment at not getting the waves I wanted – from North to South Point, a lesser but beautiful wave at the other end of the bay, it felt somehow like a brave move: vaguely defying both the demands of fellow-travellers and the slightly more suspect ones of the surf hierarchy; they could both, I reckoned, go and do their own thing for a little while.

Paddling out at North Point's infinitely more chilled out counterpart (via some beautiful rides at a mid-point spot called Huzzar's in between), every edge instantly dissolved. The left handers were friendly and good natured and peeled along the foot of the cliffs; there, I learned the meaning of big point waves in all their beauty, and paddled back out each time with no duck dives – riding each next one back to the beach with towering views over the grey and choppy sea.

Ribeira d'Ilhas
Portugal
August 2001

The surf trip to Portugal, I now saw, had been a bridge too far. Yet both she and I had wanted it this way – had wanted the two weeks in summer in Portugal as a precursor of, and introduction to, similar lifetime routines. But, at twenty-five, I was now rapidly discovering that it was too much, too soon – even though I was reluctant to say so.

Having made such deductions, for no particular reason, after our night of revelry with a British paratrooper and his lady, my focus switched to the surf. Not in an offensive or alienating way, I hoped, but in a way that clung to it as an escape from an early retreat into convention, or the bourgeois. As a personal smoke-and-mirror: as something that might break up predictable rhythms, and give time to hang back and consider my position;

as a way to avoid being the dead fish that goes with the flow, or is borne by currents of fate.

And so I surfed every day: at beaches with appealing names such as Foz do Lizandro and Sao Juliao and Sao Lorenco, working out each one's moods. Learned to hit one at low tide and another on a high: if you flipped the equation, nothing for the day. Learned, also, local bus timetables and the drivers' qualified and slightly reluctant permissiveness of surfboards.

Thus danger then switched: the threat, now, was one of complacency: maybe things were too good. I had found surf rhythms and spots, and she was still happy; we ate cheap seafood in the cobblestoned market squares in the evenings. We listened to small acoustic bands or watched local folk festivals over sangria; I was again being outmanoeuvred, but this time by my own complacent satiation.

The siren song didn't end there: I have heard that the town of Ericeira has changed a lot since 2001, but at that time it was a mellow and groovy place, far from the bling of the Algarve. The kind of place, I was told proudly by locals, where the Portuguese themselves went on holiday: it still had a working harbour; a working class feel. Few people spoke English, and long before internet bookings existed, we knocked on doors and found pensions where ancient locals would rent a room for a week.

Yet even after having travelled to Peniche, another surf town further up the coast, the need for something else – some other dimension of adventure – remained. So the winding and slightly sketchy hike to a wave at Ribeira d'Ilhas suited: for maybe half a kilometre along the side of a dusty Portuguese seaside highway I picked my way, day after day, down the cliff to the small surf village below.

There, one found an escapist-fantasy view of a warm water right point wave; paddling out below the bluff, the wave was always bigger than it looked from the shore. Each time I went, I tried to allow for that, but on my last mission, under grey skies and over dead still water, it was bigger still: a light blue coloured ocean in motion, tinged with darker tones from the storm that had brought the swell.

Despite appearances, there was a deep appreciation for the Portuguese sea's warmth: after winters of Irish surf (even in the Irish summer it didn't get much beyond chilly), I hadn't felt such languor since Indonesia. As a result, to surf on a blue wall of water with the face of the wave looking straight into mine – a vertical plane, that I ran my right hand through in floaty amazement, feeling the power to slow myself down depending on how deep you dragged – was a memory as much visceral as cerebral.

And so the retained image this time was of Ericeira in the distance, board shorts beneath. On that wave, it wasn't the first time that water had defied gravity and walled up and peeled before my eyes, but the first time with such volume. If the romance didn't work out at our still pretty young age – if there were many other things to be done first, and if she was already suggesting I might not be grown-up enough for what she had in mind – then at least the waves would last.

Boat Harbour with Brucey
County Sligo, Ireland
Circa Winter 2001

Living the epitome of the Irish rural surf, Brucey and I drove to a wave called the Boat Harbour. Accessible only via a farmyard, on what may or may not have been a public lane, the locals didn't seem to mind: driving past the barn and stable and homestead, we parked at the very end of the end of the road, at the edge of Europe, and beside a compact abandoned harbour built long ago.

We surfed there in deep stealth, away from the eyes of the world. At the time, it was an offbeat wave that few knew about: most had only vague ideas of how to get there, or when it broke. So it was with a feeling of complaisance – of being in the know, *au fait* – that I tacked the blue and white Rusty up and down the face of a glassy cold right-hander, as Brucey paddled over the shoulder, and as the natural harbour afforded the same protection to the waves as it once did to fishermen.

Chasms
San Diego, California
November 2003

I was, I realised as I woke, being rescued: whether I liked it or not, Pete's dawn patrols had brought structure and demands. They hadn't, ultimately, interfered with the late nights and the wild parties – merely displacing long mornings on my air mattress into afternoon siestas in the sun. But I knew he was helping, by trying to make sure I wasn't another victim of the Southern California abyss.

I had been happily living in with Richie, a half-Italian disco master and occasional surfer – a California special, a man unafraid to match a velvet smoking jacket with peroxided hair and a martini on, say, a Tuesday afternoon – in his beachside house, around a third of the way through what would turn into a three-month sojourn. He surfed, and had just split from a lady, and liked the Irish vibe.

Meanwhile, I was trying to find my feet in America after deciding – with not much else going on – to extend a surf trip after the others had gone home. Quickly and inevitably, it had degenerated into a months-long beach-party surf-disco debacle of the best kind. Yet however much the *bon vivant*, I had just enough of the surfer stamp about me by then for an old-school surfer like Richie's neighbour, Pete, to take an interest.

Pete was, in surfing terms, the real thing. The genuine article: the archetype of a sunburned and cool and lifelong surfer, who worked as a hand-to-mouth mechanic between waves. With sunglasses ever clapped to his surf-tousled hair, he chose, for some reason, to look out for me. Maybe it was because of my cool board at the time, the Pumpkin; maybe because I was surfing vast amounts at the beach break across the road instead of working. Most likely, though, it was because Pete wanted to surf with someone: as old crews dropped like flies (as they are always doing in surfing), I was, perhaps, a convenient wingman.

Whatever the reason, he would knock on the fly screen at dawn, and decant me into his very old Blue Toyota Forerunner. (Only once did I successfully feign sleep to avoid the morning plunge, and always regretted not going.) On this particular morning, we went to a wave called Chasms. Through the choice of where we went, I realise in retrospect that Pete (known to his privileged inner circle, and now to me, as Pedro) was also helping me to find my surfing groove.

One's path in the surfing realm is more natural selection than anything predetermined; at the time, though, it felt like a crushing failure when he took me to waves that didn't work out. At one, the Horseshoe, I didn't get a single wave on a cold grey-green dawn, despite Pete introducing me to the locals. When I did drop down the face on occasion, the wave had bent and angled so much – hence the name – that the curl had left me behind. I spent the rest of the Horseshoe session laying low, dejected.

But there had been other times when Pete had steered me on to better tracks. At early morning Bird Rock or even Big Rock – "Million dollar drop, hundred-dollar shoulder," Pete said – I had gotten waves. At bizarre breaks like the Sewer Pipe, also, there were some of the best rides of my surfing existence; Pete was trying to show me, maybe, that not everyone always had to be a tube rider or pipe master to become a full surfer. That the good waterman knows and feels what he is into, pushes limitations, and then pretty much leaves it at that.

And so Chasms, despite its intimidating name, suited. It was a left, and one of a series of peaks along Sunset Cliffs south of the city. (More importantly, it was another spot where Pete knew many of the crew, which always made a difference.) The particular wave that day was a towering left, on slightly bumpy water. The latter was unusual for the spot, because vast kelp beds helped to smooth out the surface on most days: but, taking off and bouncing down the face of water at six or seven in the morning, I felt on top of the world, even though nothing else (to the trained eye) was going particularly well.

I was undoubtedly partying too much with Richie and his burrachos; I was living on an air mattress beneath his fish tank. But at Chasms, the water was warm, and I had been taking off on bigger and bigger waves all morning: it was one of those vaguely reckless sessions in larger surf that, when combined with existential angst and – worse – boredom, gets curtailed only by carnage, exhaustion, or both.

Thus, between the warm water and the light wetsuit and the orange board, at that moment in time, bouncing down the face of that wave, I was a San Diego surfer. Nothing could diminish the status, except for its total transience in comparison with Pete's permanency. I had the waves and the gear – a suitably weathered wetsuit, that won respect from the hardcore surfers who had often forsaken wealth for waves – had the time, the place. And thus also the vista, as I rode, had briefly been that of commanding a view of the universe, as I raced past the dotted surfers and the inside flats and the sandstone cliffs. It was a totally unwarranted feeling of invincibility, that dissipated – though not completely – as the wave faded into the channel.

On the way home, Pete grilled me; tried to bring me back down to earth. Cross examining my infatuation with an all-American girl called Kristen up the road, he laughed at my proclamations of eternal devotion to her: reminded me not just that I had no job, but that there was also a lot of living and learning for me to do first. What was I going to do, he laughed – marry her? Yet the moment of invincibility from Chasms made me chuckle at his doubts.

Elandsbaai Memory Wipe
Western Cape, South Africa
March 2004

In the bar of the Hotel Eland, the guitars were beginning to play. Yet, as bottle after bottle of Castle or Hansa beer disappeared – along with some pizza, incongruous in an Afrikaans *dorp* – and the local farmers gathered for their Saturday night libations, the feeling of extreme giddiness slowly receded from its peak.

The long and arid drive along South Africa's west coast – *die Weskus* – to Elands Bay from Cape Town had, I knew by then, been worth it. Yet with a skiing girlfriend from Vermont and her cousin from the military who was on holiday from the Iraq War, life earlier that day had been far from perfect: not quite a low, because after all, we were headed into the desert in the sun, but a time of strain. Cape Town life, thus far, hadn't worked out.

Beyond the mind-blowing culture shocks, the city's magnificent waves seemed not to suit, either too big or too ledgy or too playful: none of them seemed like surf Mecca material, and the throwaway comments from non-surfing acquaintances that there were no waves in Cape Town – that it was too cold, too sharky – had started to accumulate. If I had wanted to spend time surfing while masquerading as a student, the sceptics asked, why hadn't I gone to Durban? Even the university over at Stellenbosch would have given better access to the point breaks of the Garden Route, they unhelpfully suggested.

And the drive up the desert coast hadn't been easy, either. After three hours of wrong turns and missteps across the desert, by the time we finally reached Elands in the early afternoon it was hard to comprehend that this was the wave I had sought: we had overshot it marginally, and from a few hundred yards up the coast it looked big and crowded and nothing special. Just another imperfect Western Cape wave, I concluded despondently.

Navigating around the end of the point a little closer, the wave looked different, though no better, close up. To my initial gloomy reaction was added fear at its apparent speed, as six-foot waves reeled along the point. And the pack of surfers, as always to tired and disoriented eyes, looked intimidating as well: looked like one of those localised point wave packs with strict hierarchies, where newcomers never got a look in. With such discouraging expectations, thus began the best surf, and possibly the best day, of life thus far.

Ever the mark of a newcomer, it spoke volumes that I paddled out in unfashionable booties: on countless later trips, I would work out that it was not just far cooler but also, far easier to enter in bare feet, picking a path gingerly across the limpet-encrusted reef (or, if in no rush, taking the scenic route from the beach at the end of the point). In Elands, as much as anywhere, there was no stigma in taking the scenic route: the extra few minutes to cruise into the line-up and check out what was happening, as well as warming up muscles, always seemed a better option than the blood and thunder glory of entering the water at the wave's source. It was a pace more in keeping with the surrounding desert, quiet and patient.

The absurd (and only partially melodramatic) part was that, after the paddle out, very few moments lodged in memory over the coming hours. This was the Elandsbaai memory wipe; a time of knowing only that rhythm was there, and sun was shining, and waves were glassy; a time of recognising only vaguely that the crowd turned out to be full of mellow Afrikaners, with one or two familiar faces in the line-up.

I had earlier spotted Matt, a benignly intense and early-grey-haired Cape Town architect I had known and surfed with in Ireland (and who had looked out for me during Africa's hazing) in the car park. This was a good day at Elands, and I was still new on the scene, so it was maybe not the best time for a local to be overly friendly with a newcomer. Yet, out of decorum and politesse he greeted me through the window of the Peugeot, though raised an eyebrow at the wartime associations of my girlfriend's cousin. But by then, more than ever all I wanted – rather than deal with my responsibility by association with distant conflicts – was surf. With a twinkle in his eye but gravitas in his voice, he warned me not to paddle for waves unless I was really going to go and strolled off.

Fortunately, the take-off at Elands, it turned out, wasn't as tricky as it had looked from the shore. What had looked like ledging elevator drops down the face were unquestionably demanding, but also had hidden cooperative sides: as I found positioning points in the surf, via the pack and the horizon – too deep and you would end up on a hollow section inside the main point, which even had its own name – the launch was still daunting, but not prohibitively so. Sure, kelp heads would still expose themselves on the inside, and the noise of detonation would increase – but the wave, in a distinctive and unexpected way, would briefly pause to let you in and set up for the turn and ride.

Magically, it was also one of those moments when the board matched the wave. My six-seven experiment, complete with high volume and a rounded nose and Ndebele-art rail design painted by Pierre's wife, seemed to glide into the line of breaking swell, each understanding the other. For a craft that had raised eyebrows and been dismissed by many surfers – in moments of doubt, sometimes even by myself – I realised it had here found its home, its *raison d'être*, as I took off on the first wave of the day.

And that is as much, bizarrely, as I can say. There are photos from the day of green backdrops; of surfers and of smiling faces; of long rides down peeling waves along the reef: images also of new and more languid styles, experimented with in the space permitted by the open green backlit faces. A retained sensation of wanting bigger and bigger and better and better waves but without burning anyone; images also of the series of black dots that marked a line on the wave rider's view of the ocean, forming into smiling heads encouraging you, or stoic visages checking your style as you raced down the line. Only those few retained images,: the way the evening desert sun set and cast a multi-coloured pink and orange gloss over the dark blue water; a lank-haired surfer paddling past me mumbling incoherently: "The waves … the sun … the colours …"

"Blissing out," Matt said to me, as he cruised on by. All those moments, for sure, but mainly just a retrospective sense of euphoria: that elusive feeling of a landmark session. Yet that is all – after the first drop, a virtual memory wipe caused by endorphins and stoke and blissing out, until the Elands Hotel beers began to restore, rather than obliterate, consciousness.

Extensions
Western Cape, South Africa
Circa 2005

It was another best day, but it didn't start out that way. Driving south with a combined girlfriend, force of nature, wildlife photographer and fellow student at the University of Cape Town's public health programme, she discovered she had forgotten her camera. She had taken to snapping waves as well as wombats, and in the Cape Point Nature Reserve, on a still and sunny South African day, there were to be both. Suitably, at a rare right-hander called Extensions (no explanation for its odd title ever found) that was said to break occasionally but only ever got really good on rare occasions, we arrived to stellar surf.

Amidst monkeys and zebras and fynbos, the surfing was with very few others on beautiful, peeling surf in the small and obscure cove. As a wave peeled underneath me, I could see my partner in crime across the moving water, sunbathing on the tip of its rocky point that formed the other end of the remote cove. But there was nothing to record the beauty: as we warmed up and ate and slept in the sun between sessions, it seemed appropriate that Extensions – a subtle, secret and mysterious sort of wave – would go unrecorded.

Farmer Burgers
Western Cape, South Africa
Circa April 2005

Sometimes, you need an escape from the escape. At a stage when surfing had come to dominate to an absurd extent, my little sister and her then-boyfriend came to visit my girlfriend and I in South Africa. From Cape Town, we drove up the coast to Elands. It was still a strange time: just a year after my father's death, it seemed as if I had lurched into scenes and situations that were knee jerk reactions, rather than careful strategies.

Because of that, maybe, there was an overriding need to surf more: to test the patience of everyone involved, to see if it was me or them that was off track. So when Elands went flat, the only option was to go deeper into the desert: up the coast to a wave amusingly called Farmer Burgers, which broke on smaller days.

There, the waves were good. Breaking fast but clear, they were neither too big nor too small, but did strange things on the side of the desert road. As they mutated and uncoiled, the first drop down the face of the wave required a second drop, into a wave within a wave. It was a technical place, I guiltily knew, that not everyone would enjoy.

But I was programmed to do nothing else, and so paddled out and caught many waves. Yet the sensation was a strange one: beyond showmanship and exercise and sun and surf, distress lurked. I half-knew I was both being selfish and using surf as an escape, and thus felt internal pressure and queasiness in the very zone that was supposed to drive such sensations away. Too much of a good thing can be bad – I knew that others would probably rather be somewhere else; knew also, in that small bay – with all eyes just fifty yards away – that the misuse of surfing as an escape from reality was being comically exposed.

Darkness Falls on Thanksgiving
Ocean Beach, San Francisco, California
November 2015

Gradually, night was falling. In America, on certain rare days and times no one surfs: I was the last one out on Thanksgiving at Ocean Beach, being pinned inside by lines of white water that were becoming harder and harder to punch through, just as they equally became brighter and brighter against the purple-black ocean and sky.

When finally outside in calmer waters, the waves were breaking more and more unpredictably in the near-darkness, their faces catching the moonlight as they arced up to break – the only way to locate them. Exhausted, cold, I eventually paddled in to go, only slightly late, to Willi's Thanksgiving dinner. Still in a stage of counter-culture revolution, this mixture of styles – respectful of tradition, delayed by surfing – seemed, at the time, the way to go. Either way, I was welcomed, even though I had already had the rarest of feasts: to surf good Ocean Beach alone.

The Kick-Out
Various Places
Various Dates

As surfing advances, so too do its flourishes. But nothing can ever, will ever, match the total chaotic freedom of the airborne kick-out. Where super-hot surfers try flips and airs and other moves, there is a *je ne sais quoi* at flying through the air at the end of a wave, at full speed and with the greatest of ease, with board and leash somewhere in the ether beside you. Even the pros sometimes do it; an expression of *espliegerie* and *joie de vivre*, celebration and relief. Having often been shrouded from view by the breaking wave, the kick-out is also a bit of showing off: a demonstration that one had made it all the way inside, and that disappearance hadn't meant failure – *au contraire.*

As the waves got bigger for me over the years, so too did the kick outs, until eventually beginning to feel like events in themselves. At times, and on bigger waves, the gravity-defying lurch would feel so high and prolonged and dramatic as to be almost dangerous in its thrill. There, suspended ten feet above the back of the wave, with a flying board beside, the troubles of the world seemed far away and the water a long, long way down.

Molten sunlit glass at Farmer Burgers; good times ahead: Foz de Lozandro, Portugal; die Weskus.

Adversity

Not your average tour guide. Richie points the way at Bustops.

They say it is adventure rightly viewed. They say that it should be embraced, reframed, interpreted differently: the wise say that it should never get you down. That adversity is a test of character, and that if it doesn't kill you it will make you stronger; that it is something, like machismo, to be sought out and conquered – slaying dragons, roughing it, Darwinist.

Some might say, also, that surfers have no right to complain about adversity: that it is inherent in surfing. Humans, out of their element, attempting acrobatics in and primacy over the unconquerable ocean, over inexorable forces of nature – isn't adversity inherent in surfing; doesn't it go without saying? Or is there another aspect – a human need for the challenges of destruction, devastation, disappointment? The stress tests – the primal instinct that makes us seek out situations far from the comfort zone – that actually makes discomfort zones sought-after commodities?

Behind all that pseudo-rationalisation, though, is the grim acceptance of one of life's, of surfing's, inescapable realities: adversity is part of the human condition. In surfing, it is not limited to waves or sharks, either: it can be at its most extreme when still on land – the stomach-churning discovery of a forgotten wetsuit or fin (or fin key) on a perfect day, with no alternative but to wait for backup on the side of the road. Car break downs, fights, broken windows – all the lows of daily life, compounded and repackaged for the surfing world.

On such occasions, sometimes solutions are found – sometimes not. On the days when there is no quick fix, no Plan B – when no spare key for the car can be found, when no spare wetsuit is available – adversity is truly epitomised, leaving scars in memory like waves that could have been.

On such occasions, also, it is hard to see any benefit – maybe because there isn't any: striving, maybe, to swear to yourself never to let such occasions happen again? Good luck with that …

the solemn oaths that such dramas will never, ever be repeated: that spare keys will always be carried; that you will never lose your towel on a road trip again – ever. But, mostly, the moment is one of crushing aqua-adversity: of having broken a board, or been dashed against rocks, or half drowned.

So for each solemn pledge, each lesson learned, there seems to be a new manifestation: a new way that fate and circumstance can combine to foil and frustrate. All we can do, maybe, is to try staying one step ahead: try to live and learn, but always stay ready for the next trapdoor. Yet even with such Sisyphean possibilities, it still somehow seems – provided no permanent damage has been done – that the adversity of a surfing experience is better than the wilderness its absence would represent.

Adversity is, maybe, better than nothing: on quiet days, humans are liable to do strange things. These are the moments when fights break out, or boredom makes for trouble; when idle hands become mendacious, when anxieties are amplified. The dull days, of looking out of rainy windows waiting for something to happen; the times when graffiti artists go to work and the times when – out of something close to desperation – you plunge into the first opportunity that comes up, whether appropriate or not: relationships, jobs, whatever. No time (or even wish) to think: dive in, baby, and ask questions later.

Even on bad surf days, something has still happened when fate had ostensibly determined nothing would occur: events unfold, undocumented or unrecorded – that no one may ever hear about or see – but, through their very adversity, live on in memory.

Lost Boards
County Wicklow, Ireland
Circa October 1996

As I turned around in the back seat of the car, wondering why the noise had stopped, I was met by a unique sight: three surfboards, suspended high above the road, caught in the moment. Their bright shades and hints of neon stood out against the grey sky; for that split second, they seemed to have taken flight. Nothing could have been in greater contrast to the drabness of the commuter traffic below, or the green fields to either side.

On an early mission, the Masochist, Snukka and I had, it appeared, made the critical and horribly dangerous schoolboy error of tying down boards with bungee ropes. No one was sure whose idea it was, but by then culpability didn't matter: there was no finger of blame to be pointed, nor time for even the briefest self-reproach: just a quick and silent prayer that we weren't about to land a surfboard through someone's roof or windscreen.

The instant passed: the wind caught the boards, and their moment of stillness and silence, frozen in time, came to an end. By outrageous good luck they landed in a thicket on the shoreward side of the road; only the Cruiser had been wounded by the frame of a traffic sign. Pulling in and retracing our steps up the verge as traffic hurtled by, Snukka pointed out that the wind direction which had wafted them to the side of the road was also bellowing offshore, and therefore likely to groom the waves into better and cleaner shapes. Buoyed by this thought, with the elasticity of youth we re-tied the boards with other materials and resumed the trip.

Caught Inside at Busstops
Baja California, Mexico
Summer 1997

There was a dead dog in a plastic bag on the side of the road. No one knew quite what to say or do: this was Mexico, and they did things differently here. As we climbed, hungover, from McLain's pickup truck a wave called Bus Stops – so entitled in honour of a burned-out vehicle skeleton on the side of the road – broke at the base of the dusty Mexican cliff.

To an edgy crew, its size seemed absurd: Long lines of swell broke thunderously below, even if the prospect was made less daunting by the sun and the still, glassy conditions. But anything was better than waiting by the burned-out transit hulk, the dead dog, and the dust flowing up from the traffic hurtling by, and so we paddled out.

Deep down, I didn't want to go; I knew it would be a disaster. All around me was the blithe overconfidence of young travelling surfers, protected by innocence and beginner's luck: only McLain and Richie seemed to really understand what was happening, and they weren't saying much. Searching for space in the washed-out line-up to avoid flying boards and bodies, I paddled further down the bay, only to be caught inside in spectacular fashion: as wave after huge wave pounded the shore – ground swell power lines with elemental energy, rising from the deep – I was driven closer and closer to the brown and crumbling sandstone roadside cliffs above.

My combined bravado and withdrawal was coming at a price; here, there was no sliver of sand to retreat to. Yet the entrapment and subsequent escape – diving under sets and waiting for lulls, timing sprint paddles, taking deep breaths – were themselves events, and making it through was not just a cautionary tale but also an erstwhile cleansing. A mental and spiritual reset: by the time I reached shore again, even the memory of the dead dog had, briefly, been washed away.

Kilcummin Seagull
County Mayo, Ireland
Circa 1998

At Kilcummin, a remote and occasionally difficult Irish left-hander, I sat on the edge of the line-up. A grey ocean, under grey skies: diagonal rain stung my face, and the waves were too big and daunting and intense for me to surf, even though I badly wanted to. As if sensing my distress and vulnerability, a seagull strafed the water around me, charging towards me, squealing in the manner of one protecting her young, and then peeling off. I was cold. It was not, every indicator chorused, going to be my day.

Out of Juice at Trawee
County Sligo, Ireland
Circa 1999

Beautiful waves, glinting in the sun, had been surfed on a rare warm west of Ireland winter day. At Trawee Beach, Brucey and I had parked to let it all sink in. The car filled with an ethereal haze; the orange sun sank over the horizon; the Beatles played on the radio; the white nose of the white water floated up from the shore. Some sessions are like that: the sense of stoke and thrill lingers in one's veins and nerve endings. There is no wish to let the moment go; a trip to the pub is designed to perpetuate, rather than replace.

Trawee Beach had provided us with small peaking waves, under bright cold skies; it was a place that broke when everywhere else was flat. It also offered a long stretch of beach which only rarely became crowded; if the proverbial Russian Army appeared on the horizon, one could easily cruise down the coast and find new space for expression. Best of all, it was semi-secret, semi-secluded: access required navigating old (and notoriously unreliable) Irish road signs and a winding trip down a county lane, not to mention a *soupcon* of local knowledge.

So when – having retold our surf stories to the accompaniment of heater and radio – the car wouldn't start, no one seemed too worried. It was a sunlit evening, and endorphins deceptively suggested that nothing could ever possibly go wrong. With a sense of irrational self-belief, we laughed it off: turn off the radio, kill the heater, wait twenty minutes, and everything would be fine.

It wasn't. As evening set in and the engine remained mute the stakes rose, but not in a bad way: instead of panic, our plight became a crossword clue to decode. Adventure is adversity rightly viewed, they say, and in that overly optimistic spirit I left Brucey to hold the fort, picking my way up the long country lane to a nearby farm.

There is, in west of Ireland farming culture, often an odd juxtaposition between traditional ways of living and the (seeming) ultra-modernity of surfing that never goes away. There is always someone, out there, who is curious about the boards and the colours and the lifestyle is so at odds with the past, even if quickly dismissing it with a tip of a flat cap. Surprisingly, there is rarely hostility – at worst, bafflement and bemusement at why people should want to spend their time in the cold. In true style, therefore, the farmer – when answering a cagey knock on his door – didn't hesitate. As if he had been waiting for the moment – maybe he had – he wasted no time in backing his tractor down the lane and to the rescue, pausing only to disengage some lethal looking agricultural equipment from its back.

Without any haste, as the sun set, he towed us up the lane, all the while exactly calibrating speed to allow for the rolling start the car needed. With my capacity now at a lower ebb – drained and dizzy after the search for the farmer – Brucey took the wheel, and we eventually heard the magical sound of an engine coming to life. The battery, the farmer assured us (probably silently staggered by our incapacity), would now charge itself.

Back in McGowan's Pub in Easkey, a small and discreet surfer's watering hole without even a sign outside to proclaim its presence, we recounted the day to fellow surfers. Tales of the blissing out of sunlit waves and philosophical meanderings afterwards; Brucey's near panic at the initial situation, juxtaposed with my carelessness; the search for the farmer and the switch in our *sang froid* as the rolling starts got too tricky for me. In retrospect, it had been a bizarre kaleidoscope of sensations and situations, all compressed unexpectedly into a few hours.

No doubt there were lessons which would have to be drawn – cautionary tales: mistakes had been made; guards had been let down. We had been (to say the least) far from the quasi-military efficiency that characterised the surf missions of our peers. There was even room for a moment or two of soul-searching: I had been using the family car, possibly at an age when more grounded or wealthy mates would have had their own surf mobiles. But, at the end of the day – which it now most definitely was – none of that mattered. We had surfed sunlit waves, made it to the pub, and had a tale to tell: that was enough.

Dark Drive Home from Jeffrey's
Southern Cape, South Africa
April 2004

Surfing until as late as I could, it seemed as if there was a particularly dark green colour to the waves at J-Bay just before we left. A greyish and dark blue quality to the sky, also, as we were surfing at night: so strong was the combined aesthetic allure that there had been no choice but to stay in the water as late as possible. I was desperate to stay longer – just a few extra days – but a contest was starting, and my girlfriend, unlike me, wisely wanted to attend university lectures. I knew this would be the last chance to surf the preternatural Eastern Cape right-handers, and I was determined to internalise every last fraction of their energy and magic – to hoard experiences, for future reference.

Leaving at dawn the next day, so she could be back in Cape Town in time for class, I had however underestimated the power of the both the place and the waves. Driving home along the Garden Route, it was hard to control an impulse to give her the car and turn around and return: after a first trip away from the hectic rush of an African City – Cape Town was a caffeinated place, despite its laid-back image – Jeffrey's had resurrected spirits, life force, *joie de vivre*. Driving back home felt deeply, fundamentally wrong.

The hunger felt absurd: maybe if I had been a hot or professional surfer, it would have been understandable. Yet my wave-riding had progressed by light years even since days before, when we had driven to the Southern Cape coast from the Drakensberg Mountains and Lesotho. Seeing the change in me, she had offered to take the bus homewards from Humansdrop – a nondescript junction town and leave me to return solo. Yet, with a mixture of fear, duty, protectiveness and guilt, I lied that the waves that I had had, had been enough, and that we should leave together.

On the road, driven by such false reassurances, we made it as far as an unknown and best-unremembered beach parking lot – Herold's Bay, to be precise – somewhere halfway between Cape Town and Jeffrey's, before the proverbial walls caved in. Unable to dismiss the magical visions of J-Bay from my thoughts, regret and chagrin at having had to leave was now so overpowering that we stopped the car to sort out the tangled chain of logic and emotion that had brought us there. Increasingly irritated and impatient with my distress, she stormed out of the Peugeot to leave me to – as she put it – sort myself out.

Upset more at myself and my prevarication that at her, I too got out. Honestly meaning to close the door just loudly enough to express myself – something just beyond a slam – it caught the onshore wind and flew through its arc.

Instantly, the ancient window of the Peugeot shattered into a thousand fragments, littering the car park and the inside of the car with glass pebbles that sparkled in the streetlight-lit dusk. The nadir had been reached and passed – the moment that seemed to bely forever the laid-back surfer image. She stood, dumfounded and I felt shock and shame and bewilderment: had it been the waves of Jeffrey's, or my incapacity to process their perfection, that had been the cause? Or was it just the wind?

Not knowing quite what to do, there was silence for a few minutes: any way you looked at it, what was already going to be a long and hard drive back to Cape Town had just become longer and harder. But before I could even start to work on a black-plastic-bag-and-duct-tape solution for the missing window – an escape into logistics and engineering was a merciful relief from self-analysis – a door opened from a house across the road.

From it, a housekeeper – a Mama Africa – quietly emerged. No doubt on or below the poverty line, she was perhaps used to keeping her thoughts on the behaviour of affluent and fighting whiteys to herself. With a faint nod, but no words, she walked over to the car and with dustpan and broom swept the glass off the road.

We stood, dumbfounded. There was no noise, except the breaking of the waves and the sweep of her brush. In that instant, all of the comical ridiculousness of my needs – perhaps of my partner in crime's as well; though probably not; hers were, at least, legitimate and scholarly – came through. A moment frozen in time, never to be forgotten; a cosmic rebuke: surfing had, in a way, turned on itself. It was, maybe, a reprimand to greed, uncompromisingness, and the intensity of the acquisitive western spirit that had been, that day, more curse than blessing.

Still saying nothing, Mama finished sweeping the fragments into her dustpan and returned to her house. Had she been sent, or come voluntarily? Did this kind of thing happen here all the time? Either way, intentionally or not, she had passed impassive judgement on the scene, and emerged with the greatest dignity of all. She was the altruist and saviour, not us, the privileged couple: the door of the house clicked closed again, and we were left to stare at each other, and the space where the window had been, in the descending African darkness.

Out of Commission at the Bush Pig
Kei Mouth, Transkei, South Africa
June 2004

Looking out at a point break called Whispering Waves, I knew that it was as close to a surf as I would get that day. The devastating night in the Bush Pig had taken its toll; now, even the verdant Transkei foliage that enclosed the road seemed to threaten to attack and envelop. The prospect of taking on other forces of nature were too intense to contemplate.

Staggering back towards the hostel, I tried to piece together what had happened. The blow-out had, maybe, been coming: after a long traverse in the Peugeot from Lesotho to east London, to turn left into the Transkei – the former apartheid tribal homeland, the country within a country – was both irresistible and a bridge too far. With the road being repaved, or maybe just paved, we had rattled in the Peugeot only as far as Kei Mouth – the first town across the border – before realising that this would be as far along the Wild Coast as we would get.

There, like an Everest Camp that it would be unwise to stray above, lay the Bush Pig backpackers; run by a gnarled greybeard who looked more 18th century pirate than 20th century hotelier, we washed up on his shore. After a cruise along a surfless beach and a swim in the river mouth – watch for the men in grey suits – there was nothing else to do but hit the bar.

There, with the construction crew who were working on the same road to east London that we had just limped along, my girlfriend and I drank chartreuse – the real thing, not the mass market imitation – until our wheels fell off. Finding me increasingly giddy as my repartee with the workmen grew, she withdrew; my last memory was of attempting a Fosbury Flop over a line of bar stools.

Nothing more was recorded until the next morning: thus began the next day, or what was left of it: the spiritual Armageddon, with evening already setting in. Even the verdant and luxurious trees seemed to be creeping over and in and down, sucking up the oxygen, as I staggered along the coast. Looking out, the whispering waves merged with the white nose between my ears and the sibilance of the wind in the overwhelming vegetation: it was, it seemed to be saying, time to go home.

Garbage Dumps 360
West Coast, South Africa
Circa August 2004

It was my first experience of a surf trip the South African way. Until then, for better or for worse I had been a free agent, able to call my own tune: to drive where and when I wanted, university commitments aside. To choose which waves to surf, and how long to stay – when to eat, and when to rest. But at dawn in Cape Town I was a hamstrung passenger with my life – or at least that day of it – in their hands; with Matt, and Dan at the wheel, we set off into the desert.

Dan, Matt's younger brother, was a hot surfer. He had sponsors, was nationally fashionable, took care (unlike many of the more begoggled characters I had met) of his hair, and frequently appeared in the pages of Zig Zag, South Africa's local in-house surfing zine. He wrote articles and went on trips; had been a stand-up surfer when Matt was still a body boarder. He was intelligent and fit and witty and provocative, and all – ostensibly, to the untrained eye – to a slightly greater extent than Matt was. Yet Matt charged big waves, and read philosophy, and was an architect to Dan's businessman: on every level, the air of brotherly love combined with traces of comparison; mutual competitiveness resounded. And I was the third man in their car.

Such sibling energies are unsubtle, such related atmospheres can often be cut with a knife: perhaps for the sake of a show of unity and South African cool, or merely to show up my Irish chaos against their *veldcraft*, everything felt pretty groovy for the first leg from Cape Town to Elands. There was a very slight sense, so subtle as to be unnoticed, that each of us was doing the others a favour, and lending kudos to the trip by our presence – but that was all. Apart from that, the brothers and myself appeared to have an adamantine alliance.

Fortunately, by then I was a veteran of numerous Irish surf trips with edgy and overtired surfers. Knew how fast moods could change – when to keep a low profile, and when to shut up completely; often there weren't many other options. So when, after three hours of three surfers in a cramped car, debate arose about whether to get in at the point at Elands or travel further north to a heavier and trickier wave (intimidatingly called Garbage Dumps), I stifled my desire for the former and went with the flow.

It was on the second leg, from Elands to Dumps, the cracks in our unity began to show. The quasi-cool that had been maintained since Cape Town had been eroded by the strain of ignoring one of surfing's most cherished laws – never drive away from good waves. Who knows the exact mechanism of our angst but, one possibility was that the macho hint of surf arrogance that had coloured our ostensibly joint decision, had grated with the more sensitive Matt and, in turn, Dan was feeling the strain. At one point, so sharp was the ambient edge that a full 360-degree turn was completed on a dust road in the desert morning sun as we decided, definitely, to go back to Elands before deciding – seconds later, even more definitely – to go on.

In the end, we all got what we wanted. As we arrived at Dumps, an open-ocean left-hander with wild power and size, mine was the first sacrifice. As Matt and Dan traded huge waves, I was quickly pinned inside after mistiming a take-off; swiftly, and somewhat humiliatingly, I was engulfed in mountains of white water. From the inside, I could see them taking off in fraternal fashion on wave after giant wave, inhabiting a different planet to the one I was on, and with familial unity again restored.

With the brothers chilled after the first surf, a return to Elands met with no dissent, mainly because there was no room left for other choices. Barely stopping to eat, the hectic energy of our morning had been corralled but not dissipated: our only way to regain equilibrium now was to go straight to the point and surf there as well. There was no time to think it through, nor any need to – our overriding imperative was for action and justification, redemption and best-of-both, and surfing a double-header at both breaks was the only way it could be achieved.

Thanks to reeling left-hand point waves at Elands, honour was satisfied on all sides – even mine. Only then could each of us breathe and relax; only then could the sense of competitive urgency, primacy, and points-to-prove be dissipated. Only then, more importantly, was it deemed a good time to rest: careless now of the consequences and sidelong glances of disgust, I ate two re-heated meat pies and some crisps from the township shop at Elands, and we prepared for the third session.

In the afternoon, the waves continued to improve, and the feared crowds that had prompted my unspoken wish to surf there earlier in the day never materialised. Tired and drained from Garbage Dumps – not to mention from the early start, and the drama that had accompanied us up the coast – there are glorious recollections of surfing reeling lefthanders past the once-sceptical but now intensely groovy eyes of Dan and Matt.

Doughmore
County Clare, Ireland
December 2004

It was doomed from the start. Before even arriving at the coastal New Year's Eve party, I had already stepped on toes by riding cross-country, and only quasi-legally, in the back of the Barrel Searcher's truck. To some of the more sensitive among us, as a result, I was consequently seen as a roving and loose cannon – one who represented potentially insidious threats to security, stability and bourgeois values.

A heavy night of wild drinking with the Barrel Searcher and others did little to help the situation; when we prepared to leave for a surf recon up and down the coast, we were more decanted than bundled into the car. It was the middle of the Irish winter and no time to be playing games, yet we had drunk and danced through the night; the only saving grace was that the antics of fellow surfers had been just as extreme as my own.

Far south of Lahinch – the surf town where we were staying in a party-driven, off-season holiday home – lay Doughmore Beach. There, we found perfect waves, with the tide high enough to manage the swell. There it was also that I discovered, in the cold and the rain, that I had left my wetsuit back at the house. And so there it was that I waited, in the waving grasses of the verge of a windswept country lane, while the others surfed.

Hours later, Brucey eventually arrived with my kit – with the others surfed out, we entered the water as the Irish evening winter skies darkened; as the tide was draining. Yet, with the change in conditions came also a grotesque evolution in the shape and speed of the waves. Before our eyes, the swell morphed from the smooth and playful peaks I had watched the others surf into long lines of close outs, breaking with venom – without direction, or a curl – all the way along the beach. To add to the confusion, the swell was breaking into shallower and shallower water, and further and further out to sea; strange currents and eddies swirled in the line-up, leaving me dizzy and edgy.

We returned late, unsatisfied. Everyone else had had their share of waves except for us; everyone else had settled down for the evening and were relating tales of good waves or opening beers after a post-surf feast to satisfy rabid appetites. By contrast, my afternoon had been spent pacing the side of an Irish country road; I was underfed, overtired, and had found no waves; had, overall, done little to enhance my reputation. Perhaps some would say that some kind of justice for my loose ways the night before had been done, and that karma had kicked in to settle some old scores.

Lost Keys at Dunes
Cape Town, South Africa
Circa September 2005

I sat, smiling smugly: perched on my board on a very small and very hot day at the Dunes, such satisfaction had, I reckoned, been hard earned. There had been a year of graft to get to this point, which was ironically deeply reductionist: the right board and right wetsuit; a working car, and money for petrol. A nice place to stay; nearly finished my degree at the university; injury-free; a few good mates. And, above all, enough *savoir-faire* to know where and when the waves were coming – to be on it when they arrived.

Enough knowledge, as well, to laugh to myself at the schoolboy errors that so often characterise the surfing learning curve in a new place. Enough trial and error, I floatingly reflected, to know that car key holders in wetsuit are notoriously unreliable; that even the Velcro pockets provided in leashes occasionally let valuables slip away. But I knew also that conventional key stashes are subject to wily eyes in places like Cape Town, and that oversights or shortcuts can too often leave one with no ride home.

At Dunes, though, I knew every base was covered. In the middle of a vast and empty beach, there was little danger of theft or stealth; the shelter of a small log (a section of tree trunk, washed up on to the beach) seemed the ideal covert. Impossible to be either covered by sand or shifted by the wind, I had earlier eased the keys to the Peugeot under its flaking bark and beneath the sand. Ever cautious, even with my newfound *veldcraft*, I took another look around – no one, nothing, just sun and sea, sand and sky – before plunging into the ocean.

Hyper-vigilantly – South Africa can make you twitchy – I still turned for an occasional glimpse of the tree trunk in between waves: you could never be too careful in Cape Town. But when – between holding careful backside lines along surprisingly hollow curls – a *bakkie* cruised slowly along the sands with official looking markings, I didn't comprehend the threat. Had no way of realising that it was a rogue forestry and environment truck, from Cape Town City Council, there to conduct its once-in–a-blue-moon and spontaneous clearing of flotsam.

From the moment it appeared, there was, ironically, no rush. I knew intuitively and without doubt that the trunk would be taken; knew equally that shouting and waving in the blinding sun from the ocean would do no good. Knew that they would be out of reach by the time I got in; knew that there was only a slim hope of finding some kind of indentation on the shifting sands where the tree trunk had been: the keys were, in a kind of Schrodinger's Cat way, already gone. On an increasingly hot afternoon, I was more torn between the need to address looming survivalist realities and the wish to continue surfing.

Eventually – realising that there might be gravitas to the situation – I gave in, paddled in, began to comb the sands. Ironically, that was in retrospect the worst thing anyone could have done: there was no hope of retrieval, and the search itself was tiring and dehydrating. Eventually – thirsty, sunburned, and slightly delirious – I trekked the half-hour along the beach towards the Peugeot to find out what was going to happen next.

Somewhat predictably, the answer was nothing: even if I had broken my own window to get into the car (I had seen a South African do a round trip from Elands to Cape Town, two hours each way, to avoid breaking into his Porsche), there was no way of getting its ancient ignition started without a key. Not wanting to reveal my vulnerability by discussing the situation with strangers who didn't look all that interested anyway (apart from their suspicion that I was a potential car thief), there was no choice but to go and wake Matt.

That was, at the time, a last resort: a deep and driven worker who rose at five and surfed at all other times, I had learned that his Sunday afternoons were sacred. As for many others, it was his chance to recover lost sleep and escape from the work before the Sisyphean routine started again: there was no need for any do-not-disturb signs, as every element of his life and style and rhetoric pointed so clearly towards the sanctity of those precious hours. Yet I had no phone, and his cottage was close to a wave called the Hoek, not far from the Dunes parking lot: with what seemed like no other choice – wetsuit peeled to waist, and my surfboard-carrying arm aching – I picked a barefoot path along the hot bitumen, and tried his doorbell.

Naturally, there was nothing: his sleep was so deep that neither repeated ringing nor the door knocker worked. My only consolation was knowing he wasn't merely avoiding me: in the initial months, he had let me find my own feet in an in-at-the-deep-end, sink or swim style, yet we had since reached other stages of respect for each other. Nonetheless, it was a humiliating scene in South Africa – a place where all of the privileges that the haves have means that there is very little sympathy when human error creeps in.

Beginning to now look like a potential house as well as car thief, as a last resort I walked around into the garden; called as gently as I could with a parched throat in his bedroom window. Hearing a muffled groan, I knew that was it: the Rubicon had been passed, the deed done; he had been roused; there was no going back. To illustrate that it wasn't a social call, I went straight from my croak of his name to the explanation, without too my greetings in between.

It was, maybe, a pivotal moment. But, as I held my breath, instead of anguish or rage there was genuine concern healthily diluted with laughter. After giving me a towel and some of his clothes, we stopped at a petrol station minutes later to buy a Mars bar and a can of Coke, which at the time seemed to both of us the best solution to my dodgy state of health.

From there, we proceeded to the Peugeot's mechanic, Jerome de Barthus, in his quasi-industrial zone called the Blue Route – the other side of the Silvermine Mountain. It was a place I had frequented (those interested in fixing 1983 Peugeots were hard to find; in South Africa it was either high-end dealerships or bush mechanics), but a neglected industrial neighbourhood that Matt, a lifelong Capetonian, could hardly believe existed. He had, he said as we drove back with Jerome's master key, gained from the drive. If something in my smugness had annoyed the gods earlier that day, I reflected, all now appeared to have been forgiven.

Drilled at "The 5"
Cape Town, South Africa
Circa October 2005

They said that, at 365, due to its tight-knit seaweed beds, boards had been lost and never resurfaced. I wasn't so sure about that, but knew the South African bull kelp – like anything in South Africa – wasn't to be trifled with: its bulbous strands were not only engulfing but absurdly strong, like a hundred brown arms trying to stop you from leaving an unwanted embrace.

I could see their gleaming heads on the inside as I took off; 365, etymology unknown, is a wave that mutates unrecognisably with tide, and proceeds from smooth and easy to ledging and intimidating according to time of day. My wave that day, as I stared down at the alien-looking bulbs that lined the inside, happened to be right on the line between the two.

For the previous few minutes, others had gotten the waves they wanted: gliding and elegant take-offs, with maybe a section of surf on the inside of the break walling up and accelerating them down the coast. That was exactly what I hoped for; just one or two would be enough.

Yet even as I thought such hubristic thoughts, 365 had begun its daily evolution from high-tide dreaminess to low tide distortion. Somehow, this was the precise moment between easily surfable and intensely difficult – the one point in time when the surf changes for the day. Gliding down the face, I had felt as if I was cruising: the size of the swell behind and above me as I dropped down to the trough meant that I had time to glimpse what seemed like glances of stoke from the shoulder as I considered the options; go right or left, on its lazy peak? Try to hang back, and ride as close to the curl as I could – or sprint for the shoulder, attempt an arcing turn? Beneath the grey and still Cape Town skies, in that second anything seemed possible.

Abruptly, the moment passed. The wave, hitting the inside kelp bed (and associated rock shelf) reared up and pounced. I was now the mouse to its cat, the ball to its bat: my pleasure cruise ended as the wall of water turned inside out, breaking with thundering suddenness all at once, far beyond reach of any race to escape. The sensation was that of a rug pulled out from under me, both literally and as a figure of speech: I was, in surfing terms, too far back on a close-out – and now going to pay the price.

Distancing myself from the board – now a liability – the thundering impact into the bull kelp and sea water was only momentary, yet still echoes years later. Surfers have many descriptions for perilous or unpleasant wipe-outs: emptied or gaffed, pounded or piledriven, hammered or pinned – but in this case, drilled was the *mot juste*. Like a machine penetrating stone, the wave drove me deep under; I surfaced to see the rest of the set bearing down on me, feeling relieved only that the kelp had decided to release both me and my board. But even though I had been set free, the duel was over for the day: 365 had won, as it usually does.

Last Wave of the Day in Hawaii
North-West Shore
March 2018

In Hawaii, the Mecca of surf, things hadn't been going my way. It was my second visit there, and I had hoped that my skills and style and luck would be enhanced by past experience. On the first foray, I had been surrounded by an entourage of Irishmen for a wedding: we had paddled out to remote spots together on off days and felt Hawaiian power amidst offshore-sprayed and windy drops down warm faces. Then, there had been *esprit de corps* – Kodak courage; hungover bravery; the perceived protection of the herd.

Now – solo but for a local lady – in a quest to both rediscover those moments (albeit with less partying the night before), and to continue island-style education where I had left off, progress had been slow. Warm-up waves at mellow and sheltered Waikiki had been all but flat, and our drive to the North Shore, where the real action is, was shoehorned in at the last moment.

There, the traffic was hard to manage: after a waveless session at a benign-looking Chun's Reef (memorable only for the crowds, the unusually-high number of lady surfers, and a man who paddled out with a black piglet on the tip of his longboard), the eastbound single-lane Kam Highway was filling up fast with tourists on a weekend afternoon. With slow-moving logjams stretching all the way from Haleiwa to Sunset Beach, I was faced with an appalling decision: to wait, to change tack, or to give up.

The stakes felt high: Hawaii had been a long journey from San Francisco for just three nights, and this was my last day. To persevere might be a last chance of a good wave at one of the lesser reefs; to turn back would not only rule that out – possibly for ever – but also, more than likely, upset the half-Hawaiian, half-Californian I was travelling with. In America, I had discovered, people rarely made U-turns unless it was a life-or-death situation. Otherwise, the cultural consensus was to stick to the plan, go with the flow, and wait in the traffic – even if it took all day. Anything else would echo of Euro elitism.

But, once committed to the gamble of deciding not to endure the gridlock, there was no going back: no way that a double-U-turn could be executed without fears of condemnation of even more erratic Euro behaviour – not to mention the very, very slim possibility that anyone would let me creep back into the queue. Knowing already the wind would be wrong on the less-frequented north-western stretch of coast to which we were now driving towards, there was no choice but to check it anyway and hope for the best.

The best was rough: pulling up across the road from an airstrip and exhausted by the invidious energy-sappingness of driving, we walked barefoot across the pine needles of a roadside forest to find small, disorganised and broken up waves. Ostensibly, the place and sight were magical: refreshing wind and warm air; sunny skies, and empty beaches. Only to a surfer could such an idyll be turned into angst and self-reproach.

Not so much deciding, but more from having no choice, I paddled out anyway. Yet – having thought I was alone and expecting only to ruminate on the absurdity of the situation – out of the corner of my eye amidst the ruffled and windswept crests I caught a glimpse of a pack slightly up the beach. In Hawaii, everyone surfs, and everyone surfs well: what looked like high school or college students were gliding into wave after wave as if they had been doing it all their lives (which they probably had), transforming through their graceful skills the ugly into the beautiful.

Having little pride left to lose, I followed their lead and tried to make sense of the jumbled and shifting peaks. Once or twice, the face of the wave opened up as I rode down it, but all too quickly closed: I was lacking not just confidence, but also an x-factor of local knowledge that would somehow allow me to operate on their level of style and fluidity.

With time passing, and fearing others were by now tapping their fingers on the sand, I gave in and started to paddle towards shore. There was no real reason for leaving at that moment, apart from demoralisation; maybe there had also been just enough exercise and down time to be able to manage the drive back to Waikiki. My tank of tranquillity was at least half full again, rather than half empty, so that was something.

But Hawaii wasn't quite finished with me. At the eleventh hour, I turned to see one last wave bearing down. With nothing to lose – I was, after all, headed to shore anyway – I paddled for it, just slightly too late. Getting up to ride it anyway, emerging from the white water I expected nothing but propulsion towards the sand. Instead, to my left there was a shocking opportunity: there, the white water was receding, turning to blue-green curves, and showing through its shallow depth the white sand and black reef below in vivid detail. Setting my line, I rode over aquamarine hues and bottom contours, distorted wildly by water-light refraction, in to shore with as much grace and finesse as could be called on at short notice.

Almost puzzlingly, it had been enough. A fleeting moment of grooviness and reward that would be laughable in any other situation; a microscopic return on the time and effort and petrol the journey had required. Yet it had been witnessed, and she was pleased beneath the swaying palms; climbing the sloping beach back to where she waited, I was astonished to find myself thrilled as well. Stoke had arrived, late, via the only wave on a bad day – when, ironically, hundreds of waves on good days had been left unobserved.

No Wetsuit in Santa Cruz
California
Circa 2010

In the days of peak youth performance, there was no mistake that couldn't be rectified (though occasionally immediately cancelled by the next mistake). In Santa Cruz, not for the first time, I arrived at the destination of a surf trip realising I had forgotten a wetsuit. An hour or more in the car with Willi and Rama, followed by half an hour of searching – there are only so many places one can lose a wetsuit in a car – and this was the result: no option but to steel myself for another Doughmore experience, albeit this time with the sun shining on a California beach.

The others merely laughed: Willi was a University of California professor, and Rama the lead of a Neil Diamond tribute band; we were a motley crew, but I was unquestionably the motliest of us all. The wild excesses of the Murphia (the so-called Irish mafia) when the sun went down over San Francisco, they agreed, had to come at a price.

This had not been the first time a surf mission with Willi had misfired: through a combination of his academic dreaminess and my throbbing head from the night before, we had, just weeks before, arrived at Pacific – at least twenty minutes down the coast from San Francisco – to discover my board was no longer on the roof. We had, it appeared, balanced it on top of his without tying it down on departure; in another bizarrely benign gesture from the surf gods, we spotted it – unharmed – lying on a Golden Gate Park grass verge on the way home. My reputation, if I had one, had nonetheless suffered: in spite of the precedents and associated low expectations, on the Santa Cruz roadside their earlier nights and civilised styles had trumped again.

And rightly so – except, of course, in exceptional circumstances. And life, just then, was one long exceptional circumstance: by chance Phoenix, a lady who had once been a hippy acquaintance in Santa Cruz, cruised past along the boardwalk. A cosmic dreamer, she took to the situation immediately – sensing karma, and destiny, and unseen forces in play that had thrown us together again in an hour of need. While the other surfed, she cruised off and returned with another wetsuit.

To the mixed amazement and amusement of Willi and Rama, I paddled out to join them shortly afterwards. We caught small right-handers in the sun a little way up from the landmark break of Steamer Lane; the waves were already only of secondary importance, amidst the stories that would echo from the day amidst our micro-lore.

But there was, in spite of all the drama, still time for one more twist. Compounding and complementing my original oversight, in the rush to get back to San Francisco I contrived, somehow, to return Rama's wetsuit to Phoenix instead. It took some careful explanations to Rama – and another trip to Santa Cruz the following weekend – to explain that there was nothing malign, in play, just disorganisation and dreaminess.

Never lonely for long: a baboon shows signs of interest at Cape Point; making new friends at J-Bay; amidst the kelp at Extensions.

Macho

Matt, risking life and limb at the Dunes.

Even in the 21st century, the need to earn warrior stripes persists. Even in an era where valour and bravery and other traditional virtues have too often been replaced by equity and efficiency– in an era where brains win over strength almost every time, just as services usually win over industry in modern economics – the primal caveman instinct remains: to kick the tyres, and see how much you can do, how far you can go. How high, or how deep, or for how long: self-imposed, often absurd tests of endurance and patience.

As with anything, such machismo can manifest itself benignly or malignly. By people proving themselves by fisticuffs or bouts of drinking; by consumption of cigarettes and alcohol and the rest: each has its own element of machismo, if engaged to a sufficient extent. Tough, by being able to drive cross county, or cycle seventy kilometres in a morning, or dance all night; strong, by being able to work for ten or twelve hours a day.

Each quest is associated, perhaps, with a slight hint of nihilism combined with the steady hand and level gaze needed for Hollywood visions of heroic manhood; each requires an almost competitive test of capacity (if not sagacity). For most, at some point, a permutation of these opportunities for dragon-slaying arise and become part of the hazing and tests of character that life presents but doesn't necessarily demand – even if we imagine it does.

In short, surfing – as well as being gracious and balletic and groovy and mellow – is macho. To paddle out on bigger days or on cold days – on days when there is danger, or at places hard to access – requires the metaphorical (sometimes literal) beating of a chest. If successful, one is equipped with a glint in the eye and a tale for the pub; if wildly successful, such moments are documented and memorialised by others who can then testify to the extremism you are now capable of.

But, even if unsuccessful, merely attempting the machismo tests can do the trick. Merely by trying and failing – by falling off a surfboard at the wrong moment, or by pushing the proverbial envelope slightly harder or further than necessarily required – at least you tried. Even if you paddle in, at least you were out there: even if it is cold, at least you shiver with triumph at having exposed yourself to the elements. It is only the times when even trying is too hard – when every signpost and instinct and gut feeling demands, insists, that you stay on shore – that you risk losing face.

Without question, machismo has its own absurdity. The utility of being plunged on to rocks or shore or being held down by big waves is so low as to be invisible; the character-building aspects, or indicators of capacity in other walks of life, are laughably nebulous. More often than not (and worst of all), such gestures of valour generally go unrecognised: unlike many other systems of machismo, surfing too often takes place far from shore, when a gallant gesture is just the vague movement of a black dot in the distance.

Yet to have done it – to have attained that glint in the eye and picked up a war story or two; to have shown you could trek across the desert, for a surf or give a wry smile after spitting out a bucket of sea water after a three-wave hold down (don't ask) – is rarely regrettable. Somehow, the elevation of others' achievements in front of crowds, or on sporting fields, no longer seems so far removed – somehow, a point has been proved, a risk has been taken – even if it is only getting into a cold sea.

There is no evidence, no medal, almost never a photograph: at most, if lucky, a testimony from, or bond with, whoever went through whatever it was with you. Most times, there is only a vague *je ne sais quoi*: a tilt in the burliness of one's aura, perhaps explaining why so many such stories emanate from old-school antipodean vibes. Along with the mellow spiritual grooviness that makes up the other side of surfing, it is a potent combination.

Not being into machismo, but also not being content to sit on the side lines and worship conventional sportsmen, surfing seemed to offer the perfect compromise. An *a la carte* macho, that would carry only the risks I was comfortable with: if necessary, stories could be embellished or exaggerated, in fisherman style, to suit the demands of audience or circumstance. Unfortunately, and to my horror, surfing also demanded real tests of strength and character – no matter how much I tried to avoid them.

Paddle from Bondi to Bronte
Sydney, Australia
Circa April 2000

On a flat weekend, I reckoned I would, in a show of strength, paddle from one Sydney beach to another – maybe an hour in the sea. But as I paddled past the rocky headland from Bondi to Tamarama, the beach at Bronte looked empty: an eerie sight on a sunny day, out of keeping with the party energy I had just left.

As I closed in on shore, a surf lifesaving boat was the only other presence: as I paddled up, the bewildered looking lifeguard told me two sharks had been sighted – a ten foot hammerhead at Tamarama, and a twelve foot bull shark right there at Bronte. The beach was closed, he said, but he bemusedly supposed I should paddle in, as there was no protocol to cover arrival from sea.

Before cruising on in fear and shock, I asked him how dangerous a bull shark was. "It'd bite the bloody engine off your boat, mate," he said. Delivered in an Australian twang, it was the quote that made the surfers laugh that evening in the pub.

Broken Board at Bondi
Sydney, Australia
May 2000

The surf was big, and waves broke into shallow water, leaving sandy boils as they sucked off the beach floor. As the one in front of me detonated at exactly the wrong place, at exactly the wrong time – just two feet away, its lip hitting the water's surface with crackling force – I failed in a duck dive, and lost my board.

Underwater, amidst the maelstrom, there was a long and powerful pull to my leash as it was drawn deeper in the wave's teeth. Like a powerful dog on a lead, or a big fish on a line, the high-volume six-six pulled me back and down, until there was a strange release. Coming up for air, I already vaguely knew what had happened, even before I saw the back half of the board nearby, while the front floated reproachfully closer to shore.

I had snapped a board – a tragic and macho rite of passage that my finances and *joie de vivre* could have done without. And yet, when I returned to the apartment of rugby-playing Irishmen with the two pieces, there was interest. What had seemed to them as at best a hippy, at worst a drippy, way of spending time was now revealed as having hard edges as well.

Big Waves at Bronte
Sydney, Australia
June 2000

The biggest swell of the year arrived at Bronte Beach – an expensive Sydney suburb, occasionally raided by wave riders – and a big right-hander was now breaking in all manner of different directions in the middle of the enclosed bay. The water was dark and murky, but also glassy beneath brooding grey skies – thee was an eye-of-the-storm feeling.

For wave after wave, too often unrideable due to the stormy sea, the Barrel Searcher and I dropped down faces in the hope of finding an open canvas. More often than not, though, it was just the lurching excitement of the change in altitude in riding from top to bottom of the wave before arcing straight back up (and out again) as the close-out threatened to engulf. Standing on my board for the short moment of momentum-balanced observation that waves allow after exit off the back, the surf exploded to shoreward, and one had the feel of a matador in the ring.

Caught Inside at Crab
County Clare, Ireland
Circa 2001

Earlier in the day, Matt and Brandt – the latter a Californian studying medicine in Ireland; a hyper-intelligent ripper; one who had it all – had been visible to spectators on the distant shoreline. They were riding big waves, breaking way outside and to the left of a rocky shelf called Crab Island: the surf looked hectic, daunting and intimidating, far out to sea and past the uninhabited islet, but at least it was sunny. The rest of us waited for the swell to fade a little bit, and then began the long paddle from Doolin Pier out into the sea off the west coast of County Clare.

The island itself was – and unquestionably still is, unless human taste and capacity and planning permission or building rules have changed significantly in the last twenty years – totally uninhabited, and apart from the other surfers there was no connection with the outside world. It was probably exactly that kind of vibe that had brought some unnamed human to Crab a thousand years before, because in the middle or its blank expanse there was only one dwelling: a hermit's hut, surrounded by the brownish blackish small crabs (the same colour as the metamorphic rock) that gave the bleak and lonely and weather-beaten place its name.

Our paddle out there was long enough to spook, but not so long as to exhaust: it ended in a nice channel of deep water, which ensured both a ringside seat and an escape route from the breaking waves if that is all you needed or wanted. But the temptation with Crab – as maybe with every point wave – was to drift further up, further in. It was almost irresistible: a siren song, luring the surfer towards the energy source like a moth to a flame.

By the time we reached the back of the island and the breaking wave, the sun had gone in. Quite suddenly, it felt like night. After a few smaller waves I pissed in my wetsuit – an act which, over the years, had become my superstitious Murphy's Law predictor of a good set of waves arriving. If I wanted the swell to pick up, I relieved myself – and so it did; I paddled for the first one, and barely missed it. Yet, after having had a few good ones before, I was unworried and unhurried; I had just started to find the rhythm that indicated it would be a good day.

So there was surprise, somewhat, when turning around I saw a bigger group of waves – the rest of the set, but much bigger, maybe twice the size of its vanguard – bearing down on me. Somehow the vista was in keeping with the dualities of that day: with the way the weather had changed, and the surf had started to surge again; the way conditions had bluffed and changed direction, without showing their hand.

The next waves – as the sky became increasingly leaden, and the sea greyer and battleship-greyer – got bigger and bigger. Caught inside, the first few bands of water that rode over my head were manageable, even though their vibe was changing from playful to intense. Due to whatever bottom contours and hydrodynamics and currents were in play, when it pinned you Crab seemed to both suck one closer to the inside, while also towards the head of the point. Danger upon danger: on top of the waves, the rocks were now looming as well.

But, yet again, that wasn't the important part. It wasn't really *that* important that I ditched my board and dived, time after time, to the bottom while all the while being driven closer to the shore. Nor even that the waves started to mutate and growl – as I got close to the island's edge, I could hear them making new and different noises; a kind of malign sucking, and the water drew off the rocks – the gurgle of an emptying demonic bathtub, if you will.

As these and other strange sounds echoed, and the white water surged and the waves broke in front of me, I knew I wasn't going to die. Nonetheless, I felt primal survival instincts emerge, and briefly grasped the absurdity of my position: it was winter, and I was in the cold ocean attached to a sliver of foam off the edge of a tiny and uninhabited island, that was in turn located off a sparsely-populated stretch of a rural county.

Amidst these reflections I was carping – a rare experience: like a fish that opens its mouth wide above surface for a split second, I surfaced (when I could find the surface) and inhaled deeply before the next set bore down. It is, I can appreciate, a pretty funny thing to watch when it isn't you.

And, thus, the important part – the hoots. The cackles and howls of glee and joy and camaraderie that came from the channel, where the Barrel Searcher and others sat floating: the retained image, the moment that defined the day, were the occasional glimpses I got – between being pinned and drilled – of hooded heads tuned towards me to enjoy the show. They wouldn't let me drown – but they could see the funny side as well.

J-Bay Locals
Eastern Cape, South Africa
Circa August 2004

The latest in a series of trips to J-Bay had been going well. I had, to my disbelief, surfed a lot of waves at a fabled part of the bay called Supertubes. By now, I understood the bizarre paradox of the place: though one of the most amazing and beautiful and highly rated waves in the world, it also let you in: at the take-off on the ruler edge of swell, and as one surfed down the line it was often a friendly-faced, warm water ride – even though it would eventually and inevitably swat you like a fly.

Maybe things had, therefore, all been too good for too long. Either way, when the grey-clouded front came in, the swell stayed the same: evenly spaced lines of perfection, a surfers dream, arriving from the horizon to peel along the shore. Yet the dark clouds also gave the place a slightly moodier and pregnant edge: something was going to happen.

And so I sat in the line-up, once again, after the paddle from the keyhole in the rock I had recently dialled in. Around me, a small pack began to form. They weren't hot young rippers or dignified-but-deadly elder locals but, maybe something in between – hungry young men who knew each other, exchanging repartee from opposite ends of the line-up. Just me and them, maybe one or two scattered others; a slightly Wild West feel to the scene.

One of them in particular had been having, maybe, a bad day. He wasn't getting all the waves he wanted and, who knows, maybe had other problems on his mind as well. His steely gaze towards the horizon sat oddly with his groovy feathered hairstyle, and suggested trouble, even if nothing was said.

In the meantime, with not that many out, I continued to catch wave after wave: this was, it seemed, too much for him to take. There was no justice: who was this blow in (as I imagined him thinking of me) who wasn't even getting any kind of schooling out in the water – who had timed his sessions to avoid such intensity? Even if playing all your cards right, everyone still had to pay the piper at J-Bay.

And so with a very vague premonition of what might happen, I paddled and took off again. A nice wave: grey and smooth and slightly sunlit, and it curled up in the way that only J-Bay does. Yet while turning and beginning the ride, the local took off as well – further down the line of swell – paddling manically hard to take off on the same wave, just in front of me. No problem, I reckoned: in surfing's loose but treasured laws, I had right of way, being both on the inside (closest to the curl) and riding the wave first.

But very often in surfing, there comes a point where all the rules and regulations go out the window: when it is the law of the jungle, with no red or yellow cards to enforce; when locals rule. So I didn't really mind, all that much, about what happened next – felt shaken, but not stirred. Having completed his drop into the wave, he carved around behind me; still thinking he merely hadn't seen me, we rode on together until he turned again on the inside of the wave, back towards me, and wrapped his arms around my waist.

It was nothing violent, really – nothing that aggressive. Just a little friendly push to unbalance me – to take me out and leave him with the wave. The sensation was mainly one of shock, but also relief: always, in J-Bay, there was looming threat of a sea creature that would also like to put its arms (or fins, or teeth) around you. At least this had been a mere human.

As I came up from underwater, adrift, the wave was peeling off in front of me: I could see the back of his head and his bowed shoulders at the curl, as he disappeared towards the shore, leaving me to eat his proverbial dust. At times, I reflected, there was no refuge: even in the surf – having paddled out to escape from the tensions of life in Africa – other odd vibes and energies, new and unconnected lives and problems, could catch up with you.

On other days, I might have reacted differently. Might have paddled to the shore in outrage; maybe, if feeling bellicose, asked him what had happened. Or maybe would have sat, shaken and getting colder, for another hour waiting to regain my poise: it was just luck, I guess, that on that day there were so many waves, and so few people out, that it was just about possible to continue surfing. Even still, I felt a twinge of distress, kept my distance, lowered my gaze: I had been tuned, maybe wrongly, maybe rightly. Either way, for whatever primal reason, I wasn't going in.

Had anything good come of it – was there a lesson or a moral to be gained; a lesser evil for a greater good – I wondered as I caught more and more waves? Maybe: over the coming trips to J-Bay, I got better and better surf – even if, out of respect, maybe slightly fewer of them. Because sometimes – even if you do everything right – if you have too much going your way, they are going to get you.

Split Head at Elands
Western Cape, South Africa
Circa March 2005

As she and I took turns to drive the Land Cruiser south, back to Elands Bay, it had the feel of a failed trip. For once approaching from the north of the break thanks to the flash wheels – a loan from affluent roommates – our intention had been to try and travel further into the desert than ever before. To, if not make it to exotic-sounding Namaqualand, then at least get into the groove of the semi-mystical left-hand point waves of Donkin and Doring Bay, further up the coast.

Few pictures of these places existed, so they had a come-and-get-me allure – though said to be lower-grade waves than Elands, they were offbeat destinations, and therefore ones that irresistibly attracted. Like explorers looking for gold or new countries, such remote places and the quasi-*terra incognita* vibe seemed to hold the mercurial promise of something more than just surf.

But the attempt had failed: there had been no surf, and we had driven across empty and bizarre lunar landscapes (including a vast salt mine) more frequently than finding the wildflowers she had wanted, or the waves I sought. With tail slightly between my legs, for another day we meanderingly drove down dirt roads until Elands appeared again: what was meant to have been a thrilling expedition had turned into just another weekend in the desert.

Elands, as if sensing my indifference towards its beautiful waves and spectacular location, was itself imperfect. There was a slight chop on the surface, and the skies were low and cloudy; the water was cold, and the wind was rising from the not-bad-but-could-be-way-better angle of south-west. But there was surf, and I knew the wave's moods; half-heartedly, forgetting my good fortune at merely being there, I paddled out, determined to salvage something from the petrol money.

There were others in the line-up, but the wind was so strong as to make surfing the priority: between spray and gusts, there was little time for casual sunlit repartee. On my first wave, I had ridden it to the end, but the bumps had affected the ride: too much time had been taken up stabilising and repositioning, rather than cruising and styling. Inattentively exiting over the back and beneath the water, as I rose the wind had in the meantime scooped up the surfboard: from lying flat on the surface, it had been elevated, and now – unknown to me – was descending rail-first towards my head. At the very moment of my breaking through the surface, the full impact of the side of the board, driven by gusting winds, drove down on me like a karate chop – right between the eyes.

Unquestionably, the impact could have been worse. Could have knocked teeth out or hit me in the eye; could have cracked a cheek bone or broken a nose. Could have knocked me out, maybe, or caused some other kind of damage (perhaps it did!): instead, I felt only a sense of shock as I tried to decode what had happened. It was then that the blood appeared.

With it now gushing out of my head, the not-so-sharky waters of Elands were still the wrong place to be. Yet the paddle in remains a blur: the only image seared on memory is of a kid with a body board, making his way along the shore. As I rose from the seas on to the shallow, sloping sand, he stopped to look: his smiling face turned abruptly into a shocked frown, and he may or may not have asked me if I was all right.

It was then I realised there was more damage than I had expected. Still, there was time for a hint of playfulness: this would be a good moment to wake my girlfriend, sleeping in the car, with a gory knock on the window, that was for sure. And, in the carpark, there was also camaraderie: an Afrikaans surfer, seeing the river of red now running down my chest, stood nearby instructing and helpfully stamping on my wetsuit as I was trying to take it off. He gave us the address of the nearest doctor – up the road, in Lamberts Bay – and how to get there: sometimes, even in the dog-eat-dog surfing world, there are elements of altruism and humanity that surprise and reassure.

On reaching Lamberts – a slightly bigger town than Elands, which wasn't hard – with a towel around my head, it was hard to know what to do next: in a largely-Afrikaans village, on a Sunday afternoon, there was no sign of the doctor – or indeed of anyone. He was eventually, after some polite enquires, located at a *braai*: there was a high probability a party had been disturbed, and he may or may not have smelled of peach brandy. But he was amiable, and he stitched me up for free.

Maybe thanks to the peach brandy, the Harry Potter lightning bolt scar is still on my forehead. But, like any surfer, I had sort of wanted a scar: it was proof of capacity and a war wound; lasting evidence of valour and physical adventure. Unfortunately, until it is explained, most tend to consider it a forehead crease representative of intellectual thought, or temperamental intensity – both of which it closely resembles – so the effect was not quite as planned.

Rugby Tackle at 365
Western Cape, South Africa
Circa August 2005

Back at 365 ("the 5", as it was known to the cognoscenti), I paddled out with Matt on a good day. There were two others out, beneath the rocky green cliffs of the south peninsula: hardly a crowd. But the waves were smooth and silky and enticing as they crossed the kelp beds, and everyone wanted the really good one when it came through. When that wave came, I sat watching from the channel, now versed in every nuance of Cape Town surfing etiquette and hierarchy, and therefore less likely to make any *faux pas*.

When Matt and a surfer from Camps Bay (a trendy and expensive surf spot, closer to town, that the south peninsula surfers regarded with contempt) took off together, side by side, it was hard to see who had right of way or priority – especially when local vibes and a sense of ownership or protection of local oceanic resources were added to the equation. The split second situation was made even more complex when Matt's state of being – still recovering from a lost beau – was taken into account: in that moment, it was hard to say where nebulous protocols ended, and raw emotion began.

As I looked across at them both dropping down the oily face, neck and neck, something new happened: Matt, without even bothering to shout his transient rival off the wave, launched himself in a rugby tackle off his board and on to the other surfer. Momentarily frozen in time in his mid-air hybrid sporting innovation, time then started again, and the wave ended for both of them with a splash.

Such events were not totally unusual in Cape Town: Matt had a story of how two big-wave riders on a critical wave at the Dunes tangled over a wave, and the offender had smugly gone in. Minutes later, his protagonist paddled in as well; jogged down the beach after the smug one; reached the house when the latter was showering; burst through the curtain, also with a rugby tackle.

South African surfing is thus largely self-regulating: what in other places might be a hanging matter was breezed over in Cape Town, much as it might be in Australia or Ireland. To have complained to authorities in either case would only have brought ridicule – particularly in the faces of South Africa's newly-relaxed, post-Apartheid police force. But, more importantly, one's response to such situations showed the world who you really were at that moment in time: whether you had the necessary edge to stay as cool in confrontation as in dropping down the face of a tricky wave.

So my curiosity, as I watched what was going down, was in how everyone would react. Would it escalate into a fight on the beach – would punches be thrown in the water? Would it be an arranged Wild West style face off or a spontaneous combustion; would they bewilderingly embrace the following week, or had a multi-generation blood feud just been initiated?

In the event, nothing happened: both surfers paddled back out, clearly disliking each other, after Matt had offered some unsolicited etiquette advice. Gradually, he drifted towards me, just as the Camps Bay surfers corralled in their own section of the ocean. Yet he didn't seek moral support, or even conversation: beyond a dismissive comment, nothing else was said. He knew that the event spoke as much of his own distress as the others lack of territorial manners; maybe felt that, though he was in the right, on another day he might have let it slip by.

Kleinsee
Northern Cape, South Africa
September 2005

As our *bakkie* rolled to a halt again in the red desert on the edge of the Kalahari, no one spoke. Everything was left unsaid: our very slight mutual edginess; our hunger and tiredness. But, most of all, our need for the waves to come together: the stakes were too high now for them not to. If they didn't, Kleinsee would be forever a dark name, a curse on our memories.

With Matt at the wheel of the pickup truck, we had driven six hours north from Cape Town to the Afrikaans stronghold of Springbok in the Northern Cape Province. Turning west there, we crossed an expanse of red desert without cell phone coverage or marked roads, proceeding only on the vague and slightly stoned directions provided by Rocky Dreyer, a long-haired and far-out local. Thanks to an intro from the Cape Town surf mafia, on the phone he had told us of his underwater diamond vacuuming operation off the private de Beers Namaqualand coast – but, more importantly, about the waves he surfed in between. Told us how to get there, and that there would be a party, and to come on up.

But Rocky's vague directions and our desert green horns had led us in circles, and it took us hours to reach the inexplicably named Brazil Farm. There, we were greeted by a gangly and bespectacled Afrikaans man memorably named Floors Brandt, who gave us passes to enter the prohibited and supposedly diamond-encrusted coast. There, we found only a bizarre looking wave called the Boiler, christened on account of the gurgling bubbles that peppered its inside section. Not a great wave, and definitely not worth a six-hour drive.

After I had gotten into the sea just to get wet – and failed to get any good waves – we set up our tents and drove along the coast to a break called Paradise. There, en route to small sectioning surf, the *bakkie* got bogged: even the last *joie de vivre* which the trip had given me, as an outsider and an adventurer quasi-tourist, was starting to dry up; Matt's had already evaporated. As we used car mats and rocks to pry the back tyres out of the sand, the trip felt more and more like it would be classed as a wash out. Inevitably, under the circumstances and via domino effects, our surf-friendship would be strained as well.

But the next day, the swell came up. From our tent we ventured further along the coast in the dawn, arriving at the uninhabited expanse of a wave called Samson's Bak, its name apparently alluding to an ancient kiln located there. An amazing and beautiful and perfect desert wave, that hardly anyone ever surfed: no one lived anywhere near, and there was no sign of an oven.

Under the sun, and between waving kelp beds and icy currents, we surfed. The rides were very, very, very good – even if only for the two hours that tide and swell and wind aligned. Each set of waves lined up like rulers and broke along the point; very long rides were possible, but the added edge of desert isolation made safe surfing the slightly higher priority. Better, out there, to kick out of the back of the ride, before it crashed on the inside, rather than risk a run in with the reef.

The waves were the only diamonds we saw. Hard-won and etched on memory, the extra-dark blue water of the north end of the *Weskus* broke beneath the ultra-dry desert air and berg winds that dried out and heated your upper body, even as you sat on the board. The few drops of water that were blown off the back of the wave as it peeled, the rainbow circles that accompanied its last rifling crash across the inside reef, were likewise dutifully recorded.

We surfed until it began to get dark; quit early, in deference to desert survival conservatism. That evening, Rocky had a whiskey-fuelled party (possibly with other substances involved for his inner circle) in a corrugated shed: there was a white scorpion on the dance floor, which the more addled partygoers were careless of. But the desert seemed no place for nocturnal risks, either: I had the usual overprotectiveness of the Euro in Africa, and Matt had recently split from a girlfriend. After a few beers, we headed back to the tents: Samson's Bak had been enough.

As we prepared to leave the next day, a group of Afrikaner men from the nearby town of Springbok – who had come to the coast to *braai* – invited us over. Our universes were too far apart to invite judgement, but the (their words) house-boy they had brought along with them to cook and clean resonated of the no-no-no old school – even if he seemed to be having a pretty good time in the sun. Our presence there was just as bewildering to them as their being there and not surfing was to us, but they were friendly and offered us peach brandy and *witblitz* and boerewors rolls. They called Matt, because of his silver-blond hair, Percy Montgomery – a metrosexual South African rugby player.

On the drive south, we laughingly discussed the change in Rocky's image when he had taken off his bushman hat at the party the night before to reveal a balding, combed-over dome: even the ultra-macho had chinks in their armour. Changing tack after a long silence, and in the ebb and flow of the serious and the absurd that every surf trip conversation entails, Matt unexpectedly said he had started and ended something on the trip, starting on the beach when I had surfed at the Boiler the day we arrived. His universe had jolted and readjusted, as he purged memories and started again. With the typical self-absorption of the surfer, I had presumed he was just watching me surf.

Headed for the chop at J-Bay; Richie demonstrates the fire walk; and yes — that is a night surfer out there ...

Esprit de Corps

It wasn't always about how big you went, so much as how big you went the night before: party time at Richie's, San Diego.

Surfing brings strange and complex bonds. For those who are not always naturally suited to extreme sociability, it is a good choice: there is sufficient time for retreat in the surfing set-up. Indeed, such mellow styles may even be an advantage, as one seeks the time and space to paddle to peaks further up (or down) the beach, and away from the pack: if that results in better waves, maybe a more low-key style has been justified. At the very least, the distracting loss of performance or focus that can come with noisy or overly jocular line-ups has been avoided.

On the flip side, surfing also brings deep bonds. The finest friendships are forged in the furnace of adversity, they say: very often, you don't have to have known a floating protagonist all that long before you are both put through a dual test of self-protection – and protecting each other – in the face of extreme weather, or unexpected changes in swell or wind or currents. Suddenly, you are – even if only briefly – mates for life.

At other times, to have surfed together isn't even necessary: to meet other surfers in pubs or at concerts, on the train or in work, is to invite an immediate and primal sizing-each-other-up response. If relevant skills and interests and tastes align – and even if they don't, but each is honest enough with the other about capacity – then the bond is there. Suddenly, there is a different conversation – a different interaction happening, floating above the white noise.

In my case, surfing *esprit de corps* was one of the pursuit's best features. Always so relaxing, so reassuring – yet, even if far from the edginess that can be induced by alcohol-driven or formalised social exchanges, it had its own demands as well. Watch what you say during long drives to the west of Ireland; learn the dynamics between other surfers; learn also, the occasional irritability to which all on such trips were victim – particularly the drivers. Above all, learn not to take any of it personally: learn that mood patterns would rise and fall according to swell, tiredness and distance travelled – and that there never was, and never will be, such a thing as a perfectly functioning surf trip.

Growing up, I had always been envious of the mason-like friendships that seemed to come with academic achievement – or with, say, spirituality, or schooling, or sport. Though anyone could be shoehorned into a greater or (much more frequently) lesser extent into many of these categories, there had been none that had felt the perfect fit: even the cast-iron lifelong friendships of schoolmates could on rare occasions be tainted by the traces of competitiveness or oversensitivity, on all sides, that had been there when first beholding each other years before.

Over years of exposure to and participation in surf culture, there was also the related concern that the better the surfers, the deeper the bond: that a really hot ripper or big-wave rider would have the equivalent of a gold pass, entitled to instant new friends, and invitations to stay, in any part of the world based on their supreme style. I wouldn't know. Yet, as time goes by and peers became more settled (and less starry-eyed) about surfing, such advantages – if they even existed – seemed to fade.

Maybe lesser bonds were enough: people to speak to in code, or look back on bizarre events with, tinged with a little *je ne sais quoi* from what you had been through together: surfers who looked out obliquely for one another, and peripherally followed other aspects of each other's history and development without demanding too much in the way of explanation.

Thus surfing bonds and their potentialities were also a passport to travel, an icebreaker in new places. But, more importantly, they were the catalysts of a series of deep (if transient) friendships, their names both forming timelines and characterising relations of easy familiarity: the K-Bay Hellmen; the Masochist and el Senor and OMA and the Barrel Searcher; Jimmy Snukka and the Tinker; McLain and Richie in San Diego. From Willi and Jan and Reed and the OB crew in San Francisco, to Brucey in Sligo, to Matt and Pat in South Africa, to Conor and Art and Eoin in Sligo and Dublin – all the way to next-gen surfers, in both America and Ireland.

In between, there were others – small bands of occasional acquaintances, at a certain time and in a certain place, that gave one the confidence and capacity to paddle out. Friends of friends, who had their own cliques – but with whom universes occasionally overlapped: with them, never quite getting to stages of familiarity and recklessness required to do cross-country or long distance trips together – let alone take big chances in the surf – but who were there when you needed them, and vice versa. And travelling surfers, also, who one welcomed and invited to stay – who, in return, invited you back (even if occasionally surprised by your arrival); and international surfers flung together at Bali, or Jeffrey's Bay, and just as much in need of a good groove with someone as you were.

From all of them, and their camaraderie, surfing goes full circle: back to a new generation of surfers at one's home break who are just as keen as their predecessors. Surfing has delivered, for me at least, a small set of rogue characters at any given point: types that have been consistently there, but ever changing – not unlike the ocean itself.

Glowing Waves at Mission Beach
San Diego California
August 1997

With a fellow traveller and surfer, Daz Ultra, I stood on Mission Beach at the end of another wild California night. Through the darkness, the surf was breaking with phosphorescence – a rare chemical reaction that lit up the breaking waves with a bright and eerie and unnatural glow. Running our hands through the water on the shore, a trail of bright light appeared. In the distance, the lights on the La Jolla headland looked like a crocodile.

The Penguin
Mission Beach, San Diego, California
June 1998

In the early days – even today – the suspicion that someone is not a real surfer, that they just say they surf, is inexorable. However much you try – the clothes and the hairstyle; the flip flops; even the photos and the war stories – the question marks still hang in the air. Because surfing is both so cool and so niche, there are many that claim it: some have a right to, others don't, But, in most cases, the need for proof – so hard to provide – remains.

With the Masochist, I was one of a very few surf claimants in San Diego. Living with a motley and wild crew of heavy drinkers, the ribald repartee of the days and nights would occasionally turn its glazed eye to surfing. Did any of us even surf, they asked?

Because of my many hours in the water each day, as well as long work shifts, I was spared the most exacting of the examinations. But for the Masochist – who spoke loudly, and often at length, about his surfing triumphs – it was a red flag to a collective bull: soon, no one believed he surfed. After all, he rarely went to the beach, and was having such a good time on land; he was so ostensibly complete and untroubled that there could be no reason for him to add something like surfing to his repertoire – no need for another string to his bow.

He wasn't an amazing surfer, any more than I was, but he was a good man. So on the day when every haggard, drunken, peanut-gallery boulevardier finally paddled out on Mission Beach en masse – and the surf went from average to quite, quite good – one didn't expect much from him, apart from his usual badinage. He was – to the eyes of both the surfers and the motley crew that had also paddled out – making a token appearance that would satisfy his critics, so he could get back to the real business of late nights and wild times.

The scene was set: under grey and still skies, the pack was dotted around a small patch in the line-up near the Mission Beach roller coaster; across the zany and dirty boardwalk, ever-populated by bikinis and board shorts, skateboards and roller skates. The Masochist, wearing a black rash vest for which there was really no need (a sure sign that he was out of touch) was looking dizzy, and already the object of scrutiny: I caught a few small ones, and was left alone.

There was, by then, only a small window for things to come together for him – I am not totally sure if he cared if they did – before the increasingly restless mob lost interest and went in. So when a peeling left appeared, it was, in a vague kind of way, make or break: any gambler would have staked their chips on loss, expecting a hungover and spectacular wipe-out, and an emergence to hilarious laughter.

Not only was he in an unfashionable rash vest, but was undoubtedly still stoned from either earlier that morning, or the night before: not only all that, but he was surfing the Penguin, an ultra-short board with (you guessed it) a picture of a penguin emblazoned on the deck, amidst black and yellow go-faster stripes. With its rigidity and its twin fins and its extreme shortness, the machine was twenty years out of date, tricky to surf, and generally regarded as more of an object of curiosity than anything functional.

Despite all that, as the wave peaked and the mob looked on, the Masochist somehow rose to his feet and surfed down the line. Ticking and tacking like a skateboard to keep the Penguin moving at the pace of the breaking curl, he stayed upright in the pocket, and surfed across and through the onlooking pack. Past watching eyes and silenced mouths, he threaded his way to the end of the wave: the ride had lasted no more than six or seven seconds, but it had come at the right time, in the right place. The Masochist, the onlookers realised, could surf.

After that, suitably, I can't remember him surfing again that summer. Swept away on a tide of grooviness and style and high energy drinking and smoking, his role was more that of competitive party boy – to be the one to come out with the fastest quips in between questionable romantic liaisons; to be the one who stayed out latest, or wore the same pair of board shorts for the most days and nights in succession. But he had faced family tragedies the year before, and I was glad that wave had set him up for the summer. After that, he could do what he liked.

Bob McTavish at Watego's
New South Wales, Australia
March 2000

At a dreamy and forgotten back beach, around the corner from the backpacker mayhem of Byron Bay, I paddled out with two Cronulla good old boys. Fit and bronzed beer-swilling Aussies (they referred to lager as "piss"), they could surf well – but, in a rare and cool way, they chose more sociable and mellow breaks such as Watego's, treating that kind of surfing as a holiday from surfing itself.

There, I caught a glimpse of trippy and surreal aquamarine views below my board; it was the first time that the multi-coloured bottom of the ocean floor had been visible in such detail as I slid by, over and above. As I paddled back out, the 'Nulla boys introduced me to Bob McTavish, an old-school surfing legend in certain circles – a good man to be able to say you had met and surfed with, if anyone was interested. Powerful and short and stocky and with a few Irish jokes up his sleeve, he and the far-out colours jointly made the day at Wategos.

Outside Corner Uluwatu
Bali, Indonesia
November 2000

In Indonesia, I had been living with, among others in our warung, a Frenchman called Johann. He was a good surfer, and a cool and enthusiastic guy; blond-haired and optimistic, he approached surfing with all of the same intensity that a competent Euro might also master windsurfing or kiteboarding. But he was stylish as well: naturally built for riding waves, and one who had put in his time on the road. He had even been to Ireland, unforgettably pronouncing a surfing town in Donegal called Bundoran as *Boon-Dor-Anne,* and was there when I climbed down the rocks one day to walk through a fabled cave leading to the quasi-mystical (but also heavily populated) surf break at Uluwatu.

There, he was catching waves with the best of them as I struggled for space and focus – but, as the swell rose, so did opportunity: there was a wave to one side called Outside Corner that broke more slowly, but also more majestically, than the inside section. Feeling the abandon of the warm water, I took off on waves that were far taller and more solid than I was and looked down the coast as I stood, upward and onwards towards other exotic places like Padang and Impossibles.

By the evening, I had surfed Uluwatu's Outside Corner in just enough style to justify my presence, and for just long enough to blow my mind, but still had room to half-wonder how Johann would pronounce its name when we got back to the warung.

The Slab (Frog Rock)
County Mayo, Ireland
Circa 2002

The framed image of the moment is beside me, which makes the recall slightly easier. It depicts Matt, still working and living in Ireland, perched on a cliff rock overlooking the surf below. He is dressed for winter, even though the sun is shining: in the background, I am riding a small wave in booties and hood, also belying the sun's apparent warmth. To complete the trifecta, Brucey was taking the picture from another spot on the cliff with (in those pre-camera phone days) a disposable Kodak.

Some of the ground is green with algae and looks treacherously slippy. There is some texture on the water but, nothing so defined as to be able to divulge which way the wind is blowing. And the wave is a small left-hand point breaking along a shallow reef, alternatively called Frog Rock (if you were old school) or the Slab (if new). And I am the lucky one: riding it on my backhand, facing the cliff with the wave peeling from left to right, and with one hand on the wall of water.

There is a lot that the picture doesn't tell: The Slab is, usually, a terrifying place. There are caves at the foot of the cliffs on the inside, and edgy stories about surfers getting trapped in them with leashes wrapped around rocks as the surf pounded through. It was – is – a wave designed for bigger and hyper-advanced surf: once it hit a certain size, say a little bit overhead, it is the kind of break where its contours become hollow and treacherous and dangerous. A double-black diamond, in skiing terms.

It was, at that particular stage, the kind of place I maybe shouldn't have been, but that Matt should. When it was big, I didn't yet have the DNA for that kind of wave: even with the ability to thread such needles in later years, there was back then no joy in the danger and risk of such rides; such places, then, would always be places of drained confidence and induced terror. Setting out that day, I didn't know any of that: just sensed it could be sketchy. But everyone had wanted to go, and I was a passenger, and so I went.

Yet there was another side to the Slab: due to its total exposure to the open ocean, it was a swell magnet on smaller days when there was no surf elsewhere; any hint of energy pulse in the water would show up and break. Such days were rare on Ireland's exposed Atlantic coast, and not what Frog Rock was built for; both the wave and its riders generally wanted danger under dark, forbidding skies. But what we were greeted with as we hiked across a barren field and down the cliff in a remote corner of County Mayo was the apogee, and that was what the camera caught: two- to three-foot waves that looked outrageously friendly and accessible, reeling along the point.

On such a day, from the rider's perspective the key was to stay in the pocket of the wave: the only point where the surf had enough power to propel. But, once there, you could relax, glide, and enjoy: the lapping sound of the water breaking behind your shoulder would become the soundtrack to a perfectly consistent curl until it got too close to the rocks, and it was time to pull out.

Who knows, then, what each of us was thinking as the picture was taken. I, for sure, have a sense of total stoke that I am riding the Slab. Even better, it is in front of an audience I respect; even better, I knew Brucey had a camera – who knows, maybe I would be entitled, like the cognoscenti, to call it Frog Rock if the right moment was captured. And there is Matt: disdainful of its small size, he had not deigned to get in but instead chose to watch. Maybe he is laughing, maybe he is too hungover: his face is turned towards the ocean; it is impossible to tell. Maybe there is resentment towards those who surfed such waves, or pity at such cheap thrills: maybe there is dismissiveness the small size of the swell, maybe there is the hint of a friendship between surfer and spectator. Or maybe he is just enjoying the sun, already surfed out.

Who knows – I have never asked him. All I know is he has the same picture that lies beside my desk and keeps it in Cape Town. I am not sure what he feels when he looks at it, but I reckon it is mostly an amused and sentimental affection for Ireland: the isolation of its waves, and its eccentric inhabitants; its sun-without-warmth, and its barren exposure to the elements.

Des Sawyer at the Point, J-Bay
Eastern Cape, South Africa
Circa June 2005

The inside point at J-Bay, many hot surfers said, was everything the very nearby wave at Supertubes was not. Easy and slow and soft and not highly rated, they said – and yet it was none of those things. The Point was, is, a beautiful and occasionally challenging wave, even if not half as intense or dangerous as its big brother up the coast. If you are a hot surfer, you won't be on the Point when conditions are right, despite its picturesque setting amidst crushed coral sands and exotic flowers. But, if you are anyone else, it is a pleasure to behold.

And so, doomed to mediocrity in spite of its excellence, the Point is a victim of its own location: had the wave existed independently on its own section of the coast, it would be alluded to in the same glowing terms as Victoria Bay (a relatively isolated right-hander that is also a convenient stopping point between Cape Town and J-Bay). Realising this, in between sessions at Supertubes I surfed there once a day; if nothing else, it was a place to unwind, with the gravitational pull of better waves nearby also sucking up many potential aggro vibes. In the same way, maybe, that towns around Los Angeles are supposedly bereft of beautiful ladies, there was an almost hippy feeling in the water at the Point.

Less adrenalised, but ultimately happier there, I also found many waves. On one evening after a session that reeked of rhythm and satiation – greedily surfing yet another one, dropping down the face and turning back up, weaving s-turns and toying with the breaking lip – an old and grey-haired man was paddling out. He was whistling between his teeth as I passed him in the dusk: was it a warning to say he was there, or something else?

As it transpired, it was enthusiasm and appreciation for obscure and out-of-date surfing aspects that I had happened upon briefly – a single-fin era flow and style. The surfer, I later discovered, was Des Sawyer: a wildly good wave rider in his day, he had the right to all plaudits required for any South African hellman or charger;

one who had the right to a Supertubes existence and a reason to become another edgy and frowning local, insisting on his share of the hyper-addictive waves on offer until he could surf no more.

Instead, maybe he had chosen a mellower path, but one that might also last longer. Not being into religion apart from a surfer's vague appreciation of higher powers, when I discovered he was a devout Christian I went back and examined the moment again: had it been just pure good vibes – was he so keen on improving lives around him that the whistle could have been for anyone, anywhere? Without a doubt – he was that cool. Though, maybe he meant it in other ways, as well: in spite of his himself, he might not have whistled quite so loud if I had fallen off.

Buffels Bay
Western Cape, South Africa
September 2005

There is, as Obi Wan Kenobi once said, always a bigger fish. When I half-heard, half-worked-out – based on a vague understanding of local conditions I had been forced to develop – that Buffels Bay was breaking, it felt like the grand finale. The culmination of two years in South Africa: the moment when it all came together, and I would gain the ultimate Cape Town surfing experience in threading the long right point waves in the city's own miniature and quixotic version of J-Bay. That the wave only broke once or twice a year, and then for at most only a few days at a time, only enhanced its allure.

By then, at least I knew where Buffels was: I had patrolled the other waves in the Cape Point Nature Reserve dozen of times over the preceding two years; had seen on occasion small waves wrap into the cove. So, when dawn-patrol-driving down with Patrick – a low-key, high-performance surfer I had met in J-Bay; the son of a rector who pursued surfing with almost fanatical devotion – and saw real, life-size lines of swell come through, I wasn't a complete stranger.

What did surprise, though, was the way the wave was breaking: the curl of the eight-foot swell began out to sea in deep water, far wide of the point. Looking out on it, it wasn't quite like J-Bay after all: not so much a perfect point as a freight train, breaking speedily and almost – rather than coming towards the shore – peeling laterally across the bay. A noble and breath-taking wave, for sure, but not of a kind I was familiar with.

Having parked the Peugeot at Kalk Bay in the pre-dawn darkness and driven the rest of the way in Patricks ancient Mazda (the Mazderati, as he called it), there was no choice but to go with the flow. I would have been happy with even one or two waves – at the chance to showcase what I had learned at J-Bay back in the Cape Town waters. But there were to be no waves for me that day.

Instead, a bizarre sequence of events unfolded. As the morning wore on and I stayed in shore observer mode, the crowd swelled exponentially. Everyone who was anyone in Cape Town surfing was there (except, of course, Pierre) either to watch or to surf. From Titch Paul at the Muizenberg surf shop to rippers, retired professionals, and the South Peninsula underground – from the Kom Skom to the NHL to the Scarbarians – the day was rapidly becoming a surreal and dream-like festival of surfing, as the car park at Buffels hit capacity. I had probably already missed my opportunity to paddle out, I realised, though it was hard to tell: maybe had I sprinted out early, straight away and on arrival, it would have been different – maybe not having been so cagey and careful and awestruck would, that time, have been better.

But maybe not. The waves were intense; it had been crowded even when Pat and I had arrived at dawn. Some days, one is destined to be an observer, though it was hard to appreciate that at the time. Instead, stoked to be on the scene but slightly downcast at being caught out of my league, I ate breakfast.

Yet even as I took out my bananas and biscuits, and despite feigning indifference and nonchalance, the Cape Town monkeys approached. With all the cars and all the people, they had sensed opportunity – one of them had only weeks before stolen (and inexplicably eaten) my sunscreen bottle at Olifants Bos, a mellow wave on the other side of the reserve. Used to them by now, I reckoned I knew how to scare them off. But today, they bared their teeth and stood their ground as I swatted uselessly at them with my surfboard sock. Today, for whatever reason, the energy was different.

Normally, when swells as big as those required for Buffels pass by Cape Town they bring storms, or weather systems, with them: as a result, most pictures of Buffels are shrouded in grey cloud. Again, not today: rattled by the monkeys, and feeling slightly edgy at not having paddled out, I watched a strange series of events unfold in bright technicolour. As the tide changed, and the surf grew more hollow – as the sun hit its zenith and blazed over the fynbos – I watched every gleaming wave being taken by microscopic-looking surfers.

The swell was by that stage perhaps double overhead in size and consisted of pure green sunlit water. As the pack grew hungrier, a surfer I knew dropped in on a wave to roars of approval from the car park – probably unheard, like football fans clapping at a television screen. He was deep inside the wave's barrel – a dangerous place to be at the best of times, let alone at giant Buffels – when another surfer (whom I also knew) dropped in on the same wave.

The latter also disappeared briefly from view, obscured by the arcing lip, but remained oblivious to the man in the tube behind him. Emerging seconds later to kick off the back of the wave, and mistakenly thinking the applause was for him, the perpetrator saluted the cheers as surfer one finally emerged on the inside. Only in Cape Town – only in surfing – could such a moment of skill and triumph turn to humiliation: it was time to paddle out.

Tentatively, I navigated the seven-two into the channel, knowing even then that I wouldn't get a wave. At best, maybe I could hook a shoulder as I had seen younger surfers do at the very end of the wave, but what would be the point – to say I had surfed Buffels Bay; to not go home empty handed? No such ruminations, for once, could help me to ease into the right position: this time, there was just too much else going on, and I became hypnotised by the surreal and gut-wrenching sights that met my eyes.

One benefit of being out there was unquestionable – from the channel, one had the best seats in the house. There, the spectator could see straight down the tube of the hollow waves as they peeled towards deeper water. Could see, also, the total precision of ultra-advanced surfing decision-making – see the almost telepathic knowledge that those in the right spot had; how those who were even fractionally too deep would pull back. It seemed, also, as if they all knew each other and each other's abilities, which no doubt augmented the sense of high-stakes balletic choreography on display.

But the imprint, this time, was of the surfers as much as the waves: from Patrick to Matt, people I had known well were no longer the ones I recognised. They hadn't – as far as I knew – been possessed by demons, or taken drugs, or become in any other way different in the hour since I had last spoken to them. But, watching them drop into vast waves, I realised how little I actually knew them (or, for that matter, the Cape Town surfing mindset) even after two years: when even bigger waves arrived, there seemed to be no difference, to them, than if it had been a normal day.

Each surfer looked comfortable and cheered on the others – except for the occasional malefactor: it was a day for Cape Town surfers, and Cape Town surfers only. Few travellers, maybe, would have gotten a wave that day, even if they had the ability, which at the time I definitely did not. From the channel, the sheer size of the curl framed their drop-ins, their eyes fixed on the shoulder. But there was also the casual ease, relaxation even, in stances – that was their badge of honour: these were the waves they had been reared on, and this was their secret power. These surfers would not, I reckoned, be fazed by much in the world – not after having lived their lives with sharks and cold water and giant surf.

As I came to terms with my true position in this new reality, I paddled in. Pat had left before I could tear myself away, and Matt (edgy earlier, but more relaxed now that he had scored the waves he wanted) drove me home. En route, he told me that he had arrived there early as well but had driven away in disgust at the crowds and surfed a nearby break called Black Rocks instead.

Only later, when the swell was peaking, did he paddle out amidst the mob and snag some of the waves of the day.

Such movements seemed to have something of the artistic temperament about them, unusual amongst the macho surf warrior culture. But as we sat in the Brass Bell pub that evening in Kalk Bay – a beachside refuge, wooden rafters creaking to the sound of the swell – to Matt, it seemed, the day hadn't been anything that special. Had it been me on those waves, there would have been champagne – but maybe that was just the view from the outside, looking in. Only the locals would know, perhaps: the hidden prices and costs and sacrifices that were being transacted that day; whether that was enough reward for a lifetime of devotion to unstable South African and Capetonian waves and lives. If it weren't, I wondered what would be: for the Buffels Bay chargers, as much as for me, it seemed as if there was always a bigger fish.

Delayed at Montara
San Mateo, California
June 2006

Upon return to America, it was hard to get a grip on the waves. After Africa, nothing seemed quite right: it was hard to establish, if it doesn't sound too dreamy, a relationship with a surf spot. So when the waves started to line up at a quasi-rural break south of San Francisco called Montara, I didn't want to come into shore. Described in an ancient California surf guide as having pop-up peaks, Montara was exactly that: a country feeling break, surrounded by coastal scrub and with small lines of swell that stood up and peeled both left and right – ones that kept you guessing, by appearing in different parts of the beach at different times.

It was enjoyable merely trying to crack the code of where the next one was coming from, an experience as much cerebral as visceral. Unfortunately, my comrade-in-arms-for-the-day had a demanding partner: increasingly edgy that he would upset her by arriving home late he pulled rank as the driver and called time on the surf. "Be right there," I half-promised, by now perhaps too used to total African freedom in surfing timetables – as well as understanding and patient partners.

Eventually, tarrying too long, pushing it too far, he began to shout and wave at me from the parking lot. The surf was so good that it had been impossible to leave, and I had after the years of Africa forgotten the deadline-driven culture and etiquette that I was returning to. It had been a triumph to surf waves well, and a chance to show off hard-earned African skills – but it was a mighty quiet drive home.

Tiredness, Paranoia and the Evening Huddle
Ocean Beach, San Francisco
October 2018

Surprisingly, we were now in a tight-knit circle under the dark grey sky, and trading waves. The group of Latino surfers had, until just before, kept to themselves on a peak further south on Noriega; now we surfed past each other, looks of acknowledgement and even the occasional stray hoot punctuating the rides.

After the sun sets, surfers' group. Often the least sociable of animals, there is a herd instinct that brings them together – and not just in the pub, or around the bonfire to trade war stories. Thus, predictably, at Ocean Beach on an October evening our previously disparate pack drifted together.

It had happened to me many times before – a brief connection with A.N. Other out the back; whatever one of the scattering of those not quite ready to go in who was floating beside you; the not-quite-satiated, the not-quite-ready-to-face-land-yet. For a few minutes, though, words are rarely exchanged, each protagonist spots the other – not just for safety and survival, but also to get a read, a triangulation point, on where to sit or take off in the fading light. Shared ideas on where the next wave is coming from: four eyes are better than two.

And so the textured, rampy right peeled off in the dusk, and my green board skated down the line; each colour – sea, board, sky –

muted, yet somehow glowing. If there were sharks in the water, everyone wisely thought the same thing and played the numbers: I am with a group, thus the odds are less that it will be me. Quite why anyone was willing to face any odds at all was a whole other question.

Consciousness returns at the Hotel Eland; innovative board carrier at Easkey; carload of trouble in the west of Ireland.

The Familiar

Far from home: Bureh Beach Surf Club, Sierra Leone.

There is, maybe, both a benign and a malign familiarity with the ocean that makes one paddle out. Benign, because a routine that has been established, tried, and tested is at your fingertips: a series of events that brings with it a series of rituals and systems and thought processes often redemptive in their sequence. But malign, in that familiarly is too often the easy, thoughtless option that borders on the absurd, if not the excessive.

Benign, also, because there are so many pleasures to be had not just in surfing, but in everything that leads up to the event – as well as its *denouement*. Every surf brings rituals: the loading of equipment, the effort to find a dry wetsuit. The walk or drive to the beach; the change; the waxing of the board. Checking leashes, stashing keys: each element has its own routine, and can be fine-tuned *ad infinitum, ad absurdum*: a preference for only suiting up the wetsuit to the waist if the sun is shining; a certain way to carry a leash to ensure it doesn't get kinked and then wrapped around your ankles when going over the falls. Each idiosyncrasy and foible are relaxing, reassuring.

Benign, also, in its smells: to a surfer, there are a range of triggers in the unique aromas of surfing. The scent of sunscreen is enough to conjure up a feeling of warmth and *bien-être* via some sort of Pavlovian response; the smell of wax can oddly reassure and calm a convulsing gut at the sight of bigger-than-expected waves. Even the smell of a wetsuit – at least one that has not been recently pissed in – can release strange and welcome chemicals into your blood stream: to the surfing nose, even the smell of resin or catalyst, or the fire water used to clean boards has its own familiarity; its own power to reset consciousness in groovier ways.

There is also benign debate, if you are lucky enough to have more than one, about board selection: there is the feel of surf craft under arm, and sand or reef under feet, on the stroll or sprint to the shore. The sunlit or cloud-toned sights and white-noise sounds of ocean and beach, ideally come spiced with smoke from early evening bonfires: each moment, even of the walk from house or car or truck to shore, brings easy familiarity – a sense of control and chill, in a chaotic and hectic world.

But there is a dark side as well: the drive to engage in the rituals of surfing when the waves are wrong, or when there are other pressing priorities, turns the smell of wax into an addictive narcotic. And there is the stomach-churning feeling, also, of being internally driven to surf when other priorities are sacrificed: moments both unpleasant, and difficult to resist, in equal measure. It is easier, almost always, to avoid the time-consuming debate over whether to go or not, and just go; to pick up the pieces at a later date, when surfing is no longer an escape route option.

Thus, like an old but fresh piece of clothing moulded to one's tastes – that is worn enough to have just the right distressed style; that fits exactly to contours; and which is usually just about to fall apart – surfing and its rituals reassure and comfort. Injury, work, travel, change, and life in general can rob us of the familiar – but usually such diversions only make a return to a surfing groove sweeter. Yet equally – like old jeans or boardshorts – the time comes for withdrawal and repair; in the same way, one's old flip flops can, if overused, become repellent objects to the untrained eye. To derive comfort only from the routines of surfing is, ultimately, a double-edged sword – but there are worse forms of addiction.

San Onofre
California
Summer 1997

At San Onofre, despite the nuclear reactor that makes up much
of its formidable backdrop, there is a taste of tolerance. No one
seems to care, no indiscretion too far-fetched: no doubt there
were fights at San-O – as with everywhere else – but never
when I went. Instead, usually under grey skies and on dead still
summer days, the waves were bathymetrically designed to be
shared, peeling quietly, unhurriedly, out of the deep and under
the wingtips of cruising pelicans. To have caused a fuss on the
grounds of protocol would have been as much an affront to the
place as a lack of aggression and passion at other spots: would
have disturbed the seagulls and the vibe, the kids and old timers.

School's Out, for Ever
County Wicklow, Ireland
June 1998

University had turned out differently than I had expected. Only
after four years of trekking in and out of libraries and lectures
could I finally draw that conclusion; until it was over, there was
always the possibility that the institution had saved the best until
last. But the final months and exams had been just as ancillary as
the rest of its structures and strictures. After the proverbial final
whistle, the memories of university would have not that much
to do with academia, and everything to do with late starts in the
mornings. Less to do with grandeur or tradition, and more to do
with romance and drunken cricket matches; virtually no academic
voice from its hallowed granite buildings would resonate, yet
almost every note from inside the cold and draughty student bars
would echo. University, ultimately, had had little to do with term
time – but everything to do with the long breaks in between, that
allowed for travel, surf, and adventure.

Yet with its end there was a kind of sentiment and attachment and vulnerability: where to now? I felt no sense of destiny; had as yet no job and no real plans. No soft landing or career-advisor next steps had been mapped out by my alma mater, any more than by myself. Thrown to the wolves, I realised it was just another day for the rest of the world. And so to mark the occasion, I drove south.

There, in the sun, I found a small wave peeling left at the north end of a cove. Under a blue sky, the weak yet ultra-chilled surf felt a fitting reward for what had been a chilled out era: though I was pleased to be finished, the sense that I had misspent at least some of the last four years on wine, women, and surfing (not to mention song) somehow coloured the moment, as well.

Afterwards, in the carpark, I met another surfer who had come down to check out the waves. Shooting the breeze, I told him as I changed out of my wetsuit that I had just finished my final university exams that day. It didn't evoke any particular response – at best, it was perhaps seen as an explanation as to why anyone would paddle out in such small surf. Yet the memory of the small lefts under the sun remains: it was somehow fitting; that was all the reward or recognition I needed.

Echoes of el Senor at Bolinas
California
Circa November 2003

Since time immemorial, since the start of my surfing life, the Masochist and I had laughed at the excesses of el Senor. With money and energy, fitness and humour, he had for a long time seemed to us an occasionally absurd model of milking the most out of life, of sucking out its very marrow. Determined to live each moment to the full in every spare second that he was out of his Big Four consulting firm cage, el Senor had a remarkable capacity to conjure adventure and excitement in the shortest spaces of time, and from the unlikeliest of circumstantial origins – the equivalent of fire from rubbing sticks. While others would retreat to television, he was a catalyst, an accelerator, and a rebuke to Irish stodginess and tradition.

Now that I was living in America, the energy of his older brother was sadly lacking. Yet perhaps there was something in the energy and opportunity of California itself that made up for his absence: when el Senor finally did arrive – following his younger brother, some years later – there was a sense of overload; as if the chemical reactions of the melting pot, combined with his seemingly infinite capacities, overload the circuits.

But this was before he was out there, and on a grey Sunday we sat in the parked car in the Ocean Beach parking lot. Perhaps in a gesture of affection and respect from his style, on an impulse we drove north: there had been no waves in San Francisco, but there was the chance of a surf at Bolinas – an hour or so over the Golden Gate Bridge. It was an expedition worthy of planning, requiring a day trip (if not a weekend), so to begin it at three in the afternoon on an autumn day had a hint of the absurd.

With only a few hours of daylight left, we arrived an hour before dark. Even then, there was a sense of early dusk as we paddled out; the waves looked dark blue, and at times almost black, in contrast to the orange of the Pumpkin. But the surf was a good one, and the board's colours stood out over the dark blue and white of the breaking curl with memorable vividness.

Afterwards, in the gathering darkness, we changed and drove back, stoked, having for once harnessed the energy and flow of America – so intense and pressurising at times – for benign ends, Senor-style.

Unnamed Beach
Tanzania
Circa Summer 2009

Over hot and golden African sands, I picked my way across the beach. As an erstwhile partner in crime lay sunning herself on the sand, I paddled past a shipwreck and into the only waves I would ever surf in Tanzania, and felt right at home. After Herculean efforts to get a surfboard from South Africa to Dar es Salaam and amidst dreamy visions of a new country and a new life, the surf was meant to be both the beginning of something magical: the icing on the cake.

Just like the broader vision, the waves actuality didn't live up to expectation: small and crumbly and infinitely forgettable wind swell broke in the unnamed bay, though the clarity of the water and a *je ne sais quoi* Indian Ocean energy compensated. It wasn't any kind of sign from the heavens, but merely a reflection of the way things were: I had, maybe, been sufficiently lucky, fate had apparently decreed, to surf there even once – in the same way I had been lucky to explore Zanzibar, meet her, and travel up and down the coast.

I had known intuitively that Tanzania – with its *karibus* and *hakuna matatas,* its easy-going vibes and tropical ambience – was the best place I had been, and possibly always would be. But jobs and circumstances didn't align; though returning many times, I never surfed there again. Like a good wave on its coast, a Tanzanian life – not to mention the lady involved – was to remain out of reach.

Bureh Beach
Sierra Leone
July 2017

It was the unlikeliest of escapades. The number of stars that had to align to produce wave-riding in Sierra Leone was galactic, astronomical: when I heard I was going there to review Ebola recovery programmes for work, surfing hadn't even seemed worth attempting, particularly for one historically logistically-challenged. Thus, no plans had been made. But into that most unprepared state arrived Freetown barroom tales of the left handers of Bureh Beach, an hour south, and there was no choice but to go.

Fortunately, in the days before getting the word on the waves – also to pass the time, and for the purposes of survival in Sierra Leone's capital – I had befriended a taxi driver called Cherno. Originally from Guinea, he had taken me from work offices to beaches to beach bars to my hotel, over and over again, during the preceding week: with a gap-toothed smile and a truly *Inshallah*, take-it-as-it comes style, he was protector and guide, confidant and advisor.

So when Cherno heard that I was a surfer, and not there just to work, his eyes lit up. Not so much for the fares he might be able to charge, but because he would be able, he said, to make my day in a cleaner and smoother way than the wild Freetown beach scene could: he had, he said, seen the effects of wave-riding on locals and expatriates, and described in charming pidgin terms his impressions of elated figures gliding across the water.

Yet as with everything in Salone, it wasn't going to be easy. Our mission would involve, Cherno said, a long drive down the coast that I was feeling only partially thrilled about. There were too many unknowns: wind and tide and swell, to name but three. How to get a board – and, even then, would it be the right one? The land mines dislodged by the rainy season; the corrupt police; Cherno's car engine – and what about the drug-addled former child solders I had met while walking home from the Freetown beach bars at night (even though one, a policeman in gold chains known as Mister Cool, had been friendly and protective). And not least – judging by the muddy chaos on land during the rainy season – how salubrious would the coastal waters of Sierra Leone be?

As a middle ground and a recon, we drove on a weekend to a rural beach. As the rain came down and we sheltered under a sagging gazebo with Coke and chips, I noticed a figure surfing. The water was grey, and the waves bad, but – improbably – he turned out to be a friendly Irishman called Seamus. He had been working there for UNICEF, he said, and happily gave me his board to catch a few. More importantly, he tipped me off: glancing around eccentrically in case anyone heard, he told me *sotto voce* that a trip to Bureh Beach the next day would not only yield accessible boards, but might even produce a little bit of swell as well.

Hedging our bets with a visit to a gorilla sanctuary the next morning – at least something would come of the trip – Cherno and I wound south along jungle quasi-roads that were in fact more rock and mud tracks – akin to riverbeds, with brown water flowing over and down – for an undefinable amount of time. Abruptly, after an hour – two hours, however long –through the shore palm trees, we saw the wave.

From our vantage point there was nothing but a group of black dots to indicate wave riders, and a strip of white extending like a fuse across our field of vision to show the contour of the breaking wave, but it was enough: here, of all places, was something familiar. Back in my element, on the beach my outlook went from cagey to maybe-this-will-actually-work-out: there, we met dreadlocked local surfers, who lent me a surprisingly new-looking board that had been donated by a far-reaching surf charity. In my unfashionable light blue swimming trunks (who cared – after all, a flash pair of boardshorts could probably feed a village, and in some parts of the world you might get mugged for them) I paddled out for the first time in west Africa.

The backdrop was dramatic: behind, the green hills of the shore rose vertiginously, a barrier of impenetrable green. Through it, there seemed no way to imagine the horrors of the war and conflict that had torn the country apart just years before; it was as much an organic shield as a deceptive natural disguise. Out to sea, the prospect was equally memorable: a wall of low hanging tropical grey cloud, vast and brooding, that spoke of storms to come.

Having ridden the last of the swell before the tide overran it – we hadn't left the gorilla sanctuary a second too soon – the sense of privilege was disorientating. Not only was I an uber-lucky international visiting their country, soon to be on the plane out and free from threats of war and disease, but I had also ridden Sierra Leone's smooth and clean left handers along a once no-go coast. Against all the odds – and in a life when in the best of places I have missed waves in easier places, even with all the right equipment and preparation – at Bureh there was surf, with only luck and Cherno and the Rastas as my guides. Unfortunately, I hadn't been the first Irishman to surf there – but there was a good chance I was the second.

The Green Bean with Jan
San Francisco, California
August 2017

The new board, like every board, was imperfect. But, this time, it was different: there was deep distress at the way it had turned out. As a result of a mistake at the glassing factory, an extra layer had been added which gave it more rigidity and weight, but also – according to the shaper, who was ever optimistic – more strength. I was unconvinced: it wasn't the colour I had hoped for, everything else felt slightly off, and for months it lay unused and ignored in the back of my pickup truck – a monument to misinvestment and folly. Though such disappointment over the ostensibly trivial was perhaps that of a spoiled child, I had invested a slice of my savings on the endeavour and felt a slight right to my chagrin.

The Green Bean, as it was later christened, also had a hard act to follow. Arriving into my world in the wake of a yellow board which had cruised through both South African and Californian waves for over a decade, there were emotional attachments affronted as well. Who was this imposter – what had the yellow board done wrong, except (just as I had) get old? When sentimental attachments to surfboards arise – as with cars or houses, or even couches and beds – there is inevitably going to be trouble. (For a time, the Barrel Searcher, only partially due to space constraints, slept with his boards in Australia).

On occasion, I had tried to try it out. Everything – in retrospect unquestionably due to the power of suggestion – felt wrong. The fin was too stiff, so I changed the fin; the leash felt too rigid – jerking my leg when it was put to use – so I changed the leash. Yet, nothing seemed to help: there was an undefinable barrier to its use and enjoyment that felt insurmountable.

It was only on a low-key, lo-fi, grey August afternoon at Ocean Beach that Jan looked it over and suggested I paddle it out. A

German surfer who managed to transcend the stereotypes and clichés of the breed – someone who knew surfing was more than just a sport or a reaction against Mitteleuropa angst – he was also, you could tell, smart. "That," he said in his authoritative Euro-English, looking me hard in the eye, "is the right board for today."

That was good enough for me. Expecting nothing – which maybe also helped – we skipped barefoot between gaps in the traffic and across the Great Highway, to paddle out on an afternoon that otherwise would have been lost forever.

Sitting on a slightly crumbly but oddly aesthetic peak between Noriega and Moraga streets, the waves gradually started to come our way. Most probably due to the wish to show off – to demonstrate I could ride any board, anywhere – I possibly paddled a little harder to get into the lines of swell when they came my way.

Taking off, there were all kinds of subtleties and tricks to the Bean that I hadn't realised: the shaper had put vee in the nose, which created a keel effect and is meant – like a boat – to allow for a faster and easier take-off by splitting the surface of the water. The wide point, also, had been shifted forward to allow increased weight and general presence further up the board, further easing early take-offs; the nose rounded so that – even if it was only a six-five – it had the glide of a far longer board.

More important, though, than all the California experimentation was its volume: it was absurdly thick, at over three inches in girth, leading to impossibility in duck diving but also the effect – hated by some surfers, loved by others – of pontooning. Like a floating harbour, the board's sensitivity to the wave's energy was amplified by buoyancy – you get the idea, though a hydro-physicist would probably put it better.

With its extra floatation came a sense of frictionlessness, and I was amazed, dropping down the face – hardly having had to paddle – that I had for so long disdained the board. What had been wrong; why had there been doubt? Some bizarre disconnect, maybe, between what I had perceived the board to be and what it actually was, only now resolved? It certainly wasn't thanks to the weather, or the waves, or even the words: under leaden grey skies, and over just-slightly-less-leaden wind-chopped lines of swell, the whole vista – apart from the green of the board – could have been captured on the monochrome spectrum of white to dark grey.

But perhaps – and not to get too mystical – someone, in this case Jan, had finally believed in the board. As a result, I gave it a chance, and had been rewarded. Almost like a living thing, and though no physical change had occurred, the board seemed to respond to a focus on its strengths and beauty. Once my mind had been attuned to what it could (rather than couldn't) do, the world was our oyster.

Flipped at Four Mile
Santa Cruz, California
February 2018

When is something over? It seems like, most times in life, there isn't always a sign. And even if there are flashing neon lights staying stop, that always seems to be a reason to keep keeping on: often one does; no harm is done. So it was with a curious and almost academic interest that I boarded the surf car with Jan and Reed – decade-younger surfers – to retrace my steps to Four Mile. It was a Santa Cruz wave that required a day trip from San Francisco and (due to an aversity to long solo drives) at least one partner in crime.

Lurking in the background, as ever, was the big picture: it had been almost impossible, in recent years, to tear myself away from the groovy ease of the Peter Pan San Francisco lifestyle: everyone who had come to visit, with the intention of saving me from myself, had ended up having such a good time that they recommended never leaving or changing anything by the time they left. For someone living in a bubble, that wasn't so helpful.

Baffled, I wondered if it would all continue *ad infinitum* with the passing of both human or structural motivators: my fortieth birthday had come and gone and nothing was changing; instead, I reckoned that maybe organic or natural signposts for the future would emerge. As someone who always left things late, who always pushed luck, there was a need to keep an eye out for such indicators – whether it was closing time in an Irish pub, or physical warning signals after too long in the sea. The trip to Four Mile, if nothing else, would thus be a test to see how both the scene, and my place in it, had changed from a decade before.

The answer was that it hadn't: nothing had changed, perhaps in itself a signal for change. Travelling with early-thirties surfers, there were the same tricky moments there had always been. In one way, that was vindication: a relief to see that all of the chaos with roof racks and collections, drop-offs and seating arrangements – the debates on where to go, and unnecessarily lengthy surf checks, and disputes on how far to drive, all amidst headaches from the night before –were not limited to my era or cronies. The fact that I was the common denominator wasn't something to be dwelt on – even this tech-era crew, with smartphones and Imprezas, were susceptible to the same absurdities.

But it wasn't the journey down that made me realise I was, maybe, replaying the same song. The coastal cruise in the sun, complete with traffic diversions, late additions to our entourage, and surfboard choice issues had all of the same good and the bad of a classic surf trip: when we arrived, even the walk down the country lane to the break was unchanged – a rarity, in an era when familiar vistas have too often upon return come under the developer's eye.

No feel of change, even at the wave itself: it broke in the same way, with the same salty characters around and the same birds above; the same cliffs and beach, seals and seaweed. There was maybe only one difference as a result of the intervening decade: I had learned not to trifle with narrow or light or thin boards if I wanted to catch waves. Instead, I patrolled the outside point and caught the waves that no one else wanted (or could get) on the Green Bean – the forgotten outside sets; the ones that walled up – and then abruptly broke – before the preferred middle and inside sections, only occasionally connecting with them.

On one such wave, I kicked out and turned to paddle towards the rocky point once again – just as ten years before. But, this time, there was no need: serendipitously, I found myself at the top of the local pack, and in pole position for a deep blue wave. As I paddled for it, missed it, and was pitched to tubular motion I heard a hoot: a good wipe-out was also just as much of a spectacle as ever.

In the moment of clarity and reflection that can come with being driven towards the reef in plumes of sub-aquatic tumult, I reflected that, perhaps, nothing might ever change. That I would be lucky if I could keep wiping out, and catching waves, and doing trips to Four Mile (or its equivalent), whatever life brought – that there was always something new on every surf mission, but the basics were reassuringly familiar. That – coupled with the parallel realisation that I hadn't necessarily been missing out on an alternate high-performance universe, had I not travelled down dizzier and more raucous paths – was worth the trip alone.

Somewhere in Tanzania; California gold at Four Mile; bovine localism at the Boat Harbour.

Crossroads

Willi and Rama consider Rockaway.

There are often false dawns. Damp squibs, or anti-climaxes: the moments of leaving a home or country, or finishing a stage of evolution, or of becoming qualified for something; the start or end of an era of life or way of being, either voluntary or coerced. Yet the inevitable edge that comes with such occasions is tied up with the excitement they bring: too often, they occur at stages of exhaustion or burn out, when the epoch is marked only by desire for rest and retreat rather than champagne or fireworks.

When surfing during or in advance or in the aftermath of life's crossroads, the waves rarely seem to care what has happened in the inorganic, mechanistic human world. If you think that the oceans are going to send in a special swell because of a birthday or a graduation, you will be sadly disappointed: surf arrives according to a range of ethereal diktats, but academic or professional or personal schedules are rarely one of them. In the same way as waiting for just one more good wave at the end of a session, one may be waiting for a while.

(There is very rarely such a thing as a last good wave in a session. Just one more good one, I would say to Willi or he to me. "You've just cursed it," went the stock reply. In the same way, one thing surfing doesn't offer is the response of nature to human will. There is, more often than not, no good last one: merely cold and darkness and the loss of stoke. In the same way, the wish for a perfect wave to bid adieu to whatever, whomever, or wherever you are leaving is equally improbable.)

Yet since I began surfing over two decades ago, almost every life event had been marked by a session. From the death of my father to graduation from college; from meeting cool people to breaking up with girlfriends to ending long sojourns in Africa. One hopes there may be other landmarks in the future that will be either toasted by or memorialised in a surf session, no matter how pitiful the waves. On days when the surf happens to be good as well, then the depth of the memory marker for the decision or event in question runs even deeper – but that is rare, and ultimately a bonus.

And surfing can also create its own crossroads: the sessions when you weren't necessarily looking for any kind of epiphany, behavioural change, or personal evolution, but it is thrust upon you. On days when seeing the shadow of a sea creature underneath your hungover feet, there is, afterwards – I can assure you – ample time and motivation for reflection, reassessment, and redirection.

In both cases, there are markers in the ocean for many of life's more dramatic stages of evolution: these are the surf sessions that become imprinted because of external rather than inherent significance; moments that will always be remembered are coloured by those contexts, and lodged in memory accordingly – no matter how bad the waves were.

Thus, for better or for worse, the times that get remembered as crossroads sessions are unique in themselves. To be out in the water at such moments – no matter how the waves are, no matter how momentous the event – has its own significance beyond the thrill of a good ride. On such occasions, surfing offers at least a pause: a reality check, and time to ensure that the Rubicon being crossed is the right one.

Sometimes, it is only when the waves come through that you realise you are making the right (or wrong) call – at a place called Kommetjie, I got a deep sense that my time in South Africa was over – but, by then, it usually doesn't matter. At other times, the crossroads session can be a suggestion of what not to do: a day of getting pinned inside with hungover nausea and hardly any waves was a stirring, even if occasionally unheeded, call to end the era of heavy college partying.

In either case – affirmation or condemnation – surfing can sometimes let us know if we are moving in the right direction: on occasions when there is no map or compass, answers can sometimes come out of the deep.

Perfect Day at Crab
County Clare, Ireland
Circa Autumn 1999

On an Irish sunny day, the small waves reeled. It was a moment of what seemed to approach perfection: glassy conditions and youth and surf and a car and a cool girlfriend, all at once. In surf speak, there were fun waves: her family had an apartment at the nearby seaside town of Lahinch; Crab Island, in front of us, was conveniently picking up the tiny remnants of swell on an otherwise flat coast.

Right place, right time. Even if the surf would be nothing to write home about, I would have surfed Crab in the sun; would have gotten predictions right, and proven possession of those twin but eternally elusive surfing virtues: luck and timing. Even the tide was cooperating, as it reduced the volume of water between swell and shore: helping the waves to break further out, and therefore at greater length, on Crab's sloping shelf.

At that moment, everything was in synch: at Crab that day, there was wave after wave. Behind the island at the top of its point, the right-handers reared and peeled in dreamy fashion. The water was warm, and even the board was right – a six-ten round nose double-ender, the Mini Mal, that felt like it had been built for the day. There was nothing more anyone could have asked for: coming in under an orange dusk, we went back to the apartment and out to dinner.

It didn't matter that the functionality of the day had been dependent on nature: the lady was pleased that I was pleased; everything looked smooth for the future. And it didn't matter, then, that I would only later discover the challenges of making choices on such shifting sands – what if the waves had been bad, or the wind had been wrong; what if a pack of angry locals had descended to dominate the swell? The moments of ultra-perfection, when all of the stars are aligned, can be deceptive

– the times when life tricks you into thinking you had reached some kind of destination, ahead of time.

Sometime later, when parting ways – she to London, me to the USA – it was a sad occasion, but also had a hint of logic and inevitability about it. There was, it seemed, no way of knowing deep truths when conditions were perfect – in the same way one could never say a wave was a certain way based on its behaviour on a certain day. I had seen Crab turn into a man-eater on other occasions – had myself felt its teeth, when caught in its maw. In the same way, maybe, the moment of perfection passed, along with the opportunities it offered. Twenty years later, it was the right choice: sometimes you can only really see the soul – one's own, or that of others – in the wind and the rain and the cold.

Enniscrone Point
County Sligo, Ireland
December 2003

I had driven to the west of Ireland with my Mum, her first time on a surf trip, soon after my Dad died. There was a long crescent beach at Enniscrone, and a swell came through at a place he had liked – close to the harbour, and close to where he had been born. The waves were good – cold and grey, but long and uncrowded, smooth and reeling. At the end of each one I would finish surfing near the arm of the harbour wall that I had walked on with him before paddling out for another, while Mum walked along the beach.

Shadows at the Dunes
Western Cape, South Africa
September 2005

Somehow, the events of the next day fit with, even flowed from, the night before. There had been something slightly off and slightly edgy about the surfing party – I was with a younger crew of Kommetjie surfers I didn't know so well, but there had been a lot of drinking anyway. Too much: towards the end of the night, the last men standing started to casually fling their glass beer bottles over the back wall of the house. After an evening of watching the clique sport of rugby, it was at best an environmentally dodgy drunken move; at worst, some kind of vague, unintentional, youthful affront to Africa itself, from within the smug confines of private property.

After a hazy night of sleep on the couch, the weekend extravaganza was to be completed, in a spirit of *esprit de corps*, by a collective surf at a beach break in Cape Town called the Dunes. It is a slightly mystical and macho spot: a long stretch of white sand between Kommetjie and Noordhoek, in the middle of which, after a trek along the sand, stand the finest and cleanest and best waves around. The kind of waves one almost had to be invited to surf, the kind of place that few outsiders would bother with: the kind of place where, if someone was going and they invited you along, you were for sure going to say yes.

Inevitably, however, there were diversions and protracted recoveries and incapacitated surfers from the night before; slowly, the surf-hungry massif from the party dwindled to just a few. Even then, going from party house to beach involved a long and hot walk, further atomising and eroding the collective. By that stage, it was every man for himself as the remainder of our posse – no more than three or four – paddled out.

In a state of mild stupor, the priority was not, for once, catching waves. Dunes is a tricky and hollow and fast breaking wave, one that demands peak condition even on small days: to try to tackle it under blazing and blinding sunlight on a busy Sunday seemed almost laughable. Simply to be in the ocean and feel its enveloping cold, its relief to a throbbing head, would be more than enough.

Gazing out to sea, sunbathing and bobbing around and trying to see if there would be a wave for a surfer sailing at half mast, I heard a hoot. It seemed at first almost surreal: an unknown surfer was paddling towards me as fast as he could, shouting with what seemed like enthusiasm. In my still slightly altered state, I assumed he was either demented or wildly happy about a ride

– in Cape Town, as in San Francisco, it was quite possibly the former. Yet as he grew closer, I could see there was something else in his eyes.

"Yassers," he said. "I've just seen a huge shark, bru." Not quite knowing how to reply, as he spread the word people started to move. Agonisingly unhurriedly, lest anyone send out a panic signal that would seem like a struggling fish and thus attract predators – but definitely not hanging about either – I had only time for a glance around before I eased shoreward.

In that moment of scoping, it is still impossible to say what I saw. Such was my state, and such the multi-hued colour of the ocean, the brightness of the sun, that the darker patch – around ten feet long – that I thought I saw a few yards away could have been anything. Could have been a kelp head, or a trick of the light; could have been a rock on the ocean floor. In my haze, I couldn't even say for sure if it was the shape or my eyes that were swimming.

Arriving at the beach, everyone was standing on the shore: no one had been hurt. The collected surfers looked oddly like stick figures in their black wetsuits against the white of the sand; no one seemed quite to know what to do in the slightly uncertain anti-climax that always accompanies acts of prevention. After a while, some paddled back out; others drifted away. Still not sure if my mind was sufficiently clear to be able to attempt the drive home – still not quite wanting the weekend to end – I stood for a while, gazing mindlessly out to sea before walking back down the beach.

When asked if I ever saw a shark in South Africa after two years of surfing there, I hesitate. It seems almost to be risking affront to the ocean to glamorise the tale; others had been badly hurt at Dunes, others also have much more vivid tales. Yet it was a shot across the bows, however one might interpret it: I didn't surf the Dunes so much after that, and only rarely on days when there were few others out. And certainly, definitely, never with a wild hangover from the night before.

Last Wave in Cape Town
Western Cape, South Africa
November 2005

After every prevaricating procrastination, my Cape Town days were ending. They had been tricky, but there was by then an element of affection: like anything that one had gotten dialled in, I felt a Stockholm-Syndrome reluctance to leave; half the effort and half the learning would, I knew, now be useless for ever.

There had been no landmark swell to signal departure. The last trip to J-Bay the week before had barely justified itself apart from a sense of achievement at having done it solo (not recommended, particularly with no radio and in a very old Peugeot). Overall, the final weeks had been quiet – not a bad thing in Africa – and I was back at Long Beach Kommetjie, the old reliable. The spot had been the scene of a hundred sessions over the two years there, yet this was one of the only ones to be imprinted on memory.

In a desperate attempt to hold on to some tangible element of Africa, I had had a bright yellow board, a high-volume six-six, shaped to take home with me. So far, there had been few chances to use it, and I doubted if there would be another one. So with Matt watching from the ablution block (as the South Africans formally call their showers), I paddled out: it was small, at best only two foot, but there were people in the water, and a little left was breaking along the cobblestones to one side of the break. Long Beach could break in maybe twenty different ways, I had learned, and this was just one manifestation.

The wave, when it came, was one of a series of those lefts; the new board still felt like an unreliable stranger, but responded to the take-off, and turned towards the face. The ride, ultimately, was nothing special – but the wave did do one unusual thing. Unexpectedly, it lined up and reeled; I just stood there and stayed in the pocket and didn't have to do anything. To surf it without really moving was enough; it was also, maybe, the only way it could have been surfed. That was just as much, I had recently begun to tell myself, a reflection of surfing well as any dazzling wave at any high-profile spot: the balance and trim required, even in that sunny grey water on a quiet and still day in Kommetjie, had its own demands.

As it continued to spin along the line, there was also a moment of glancing up to see an approving nod from Matt: peeling off with a theatrical salute at the end of a nondescript wave to mark the end of an era, I knew how lucky I had been. For sure, I knew that such a small wave would have no right to stand out in memory: knew that, even if it did, it would be no reflection of months of challenging but unforgettable times: the occasional dangers, and the adrenaline rushes.

But, in a way, the wave represented both luck and survival. Who cared, really, how it had ended? I had lived to tell the tale of what had gone before – done what I had had to do in South African surfing's ever-demanding realm for two years, sometimes reluctantly, so I guess that I might as well enjoy the final curtain call. Even Matt's kind appreciation didn't really matter either way – what had been done had been done, and that was that. I had either succeeded or failed, depending on your point of view – depending on one's definition of surfing, or life, success or failure.

And, finally, the wave was also a relief. I hadn't fallen off: had ended South Africa as cleanly as I could, and no sea creature had lurched out of the water on my last day to add an unwanted footnote to two years of invading their element. Instead, on the mellow Kommetjie day, there was no drama; barely even a breath of wind amongst the dotted surfers gathered – unknowingly and unwittingly – to mark the occasion.

But, back to land, I was pleased Matt was stoked. He greeted me with a beaming smile, saying, "Your last wave in Cape Town, bru!" Now divested of his quasi-responsibility for, and oversight of, both my adventures and misadventures, we headed to the Red Herring – a wood-panelled and firelit Noordhoek pub – to drink Namibian beers and mark the occasion.

Lissadell with the Violent Femmes
County Sligo, Ireland
December 2005

On return to Ireland after two years in South Africa, much had changed. Easy-going surfing mates had settled down, preparing to get married; just a hint of their peak responsiveness and *espliegerie* and reckless decision-making had been sanded down as a precursor to the demands that lay ahead. But there was still a little play in the system: with the Barrel Searcher and el Gordo, we drove west in the early dawn to surf a wave elegantly called Lissadell.

It was a long drive, in the back of a truck: still hazy from the night before, we closed in on the Atlantic coast in the freezing rain. Yet with interest rising as we sensed the surf, we motored down the country roads in anticipation. And then – bang! wham! bingo! – there it was: a panorama of green fields, grey skies, perfect lines of swell in front of our eyes. This was Ireland: there was surf, and when stars and conditions aligned it could compare with anywhere on earth.

Paddling out in a slightly-too-thin South African wetsuit, though, was a different ball game.: I knew that without passing the threshold of numbness and entering a less sensitised mode, I would never last. Painful at first, it was the only option available: to have gone in then would have meant no return to the surf that day. (I also didn't know where the car keys were.) Gradually, a possibly-slightly-unhealthy numbness set in, and I knew it would be all right.

Leaving the waves on the inside – mainly to keep moving, and therefore stay warm – in a display of quasi-African valour I paddled further out and up the point. There, a left-hander was breaking along with a surfer I had, bizarrely, known from years before; we laughed and traded icy waves. Out the back, the sea was of just a slightly different tone of green-grey to the sky: As the waves broke, the white water capped their lips in the light offshore wind.

Eventually I paddled in, though it was only in the carpark that it all came out: after the hyper-cold and the years of exile travel in South Africa and America; after the gravitas and ubiquitous exposure to inequality (not to mention the associated, incessant, invidious fear of crime) of the Cape Town scene was all suddenly washed away. Still in my wetsuit and almost delirious from the cold, I started to dance as the Barrel Searcher turned up the volume of The Violent Femmes' *High as a Kite* to warm us up.

The scene was abominably absurd: wet-suited surfers, dancing to the music to try and restore circulation on the Irish winter coast. With rocky-green-field-emptiness for miles around, apart from the odd bemused camper van, there was no one to disturb as the song echoed along the coast in bizarre juxtaposition to the quietness of nature. It was boorish and childish, sure, but also a moment captured in time: the passing of a period when everything had briefly become edgy and functional. Even if its days of peak brightness were less frequent, the sparkle of the old-school crew was back.

New Year's Day at Four Mile
Santa Cruz, California
January 2007

Though there had been no confirmation, the end was coming near. It had been a lukewarm Christmas with a girlfriend's family in Vermont, and America still felt too vast to negotiate: at the time, it was clear I wasn't ready for a settled life. So when the call came through from Willi to drive south to Santa Cruz on New Year's Day, I didn't hesitate – what would be, would be.

Despite the much-vaunted escapism of the surf mission, throughout the trip a lurking sense of unease remained. There was no way to shake the feeling of trouble ahead – an insidious sensation, that even sunshine and camaraderie couldn't dissolve. Only when we reached Four Mile, a mellow wave outside Santa Cruz which could get incredibly good, was there any glimmer of relief. As we wound down the farmland path with boards under arms, a truly distracting sight was revealed: four foot right-handers, peeling across the bay and smoothed out by kelpy waters; pelicans and seagulls in the air, sun in the sky.

There is just one recollection from the session, a bizarre combination of image and thought: ahead, the wave peels as I stand on my yellow board, its brightness contrasting with the muted blue-green of the ocean. There is a sense of wind and speed as the board flies across the face of the wave; its more prosaic significance lies in its being my first wave of the year.

Yet, unlike New Year's resolutions or other proclamations, the first wave of a year has no predictive value. At best, perhaps it proves that one can still surf, and has a chance of a year of waves ahead – but there has never been a satisfactory superstition linking the first ride of January with events to come: no correlation no connection between a good start and a bountiful harvest, any more than between falling off and kicking off an *annus horribilis*.

But, in this case, everything had come together: briefly, I amused myself by dreaming I was off on the right foot, even if my very presence in the line-up was most likely adding to the tumult that lay ahead. I wondered while kicking out if this was the meteorological calm before the personal storm: if it was, how long would the tempest last – how long before I would feel the light footed *joie de vivre* that stable living can, ironically, bring to surfing? In the event, it was to be many months: before the proverbial storm set in, Four Mile gave a last gasp of easy-going air; a last frictionless cruise along the face.

Missed Wave at Elands
Western Cape, South Africa
Circa 2015

At a place once known intimately, I was now just passing through: I had, during two years of living in Cape Town, come to know Elands in almost eccentric detail. I could predict, well enough, how the swell was going to be by looking at indicators close to home: could read the charts and knew who to talk to when making the call to drive into the desert. Knew the tides and winds and weather and crowds; knew about marine life, and kelp beds. Knew, also, what times of year the wave liked, and where to stay – knew the best route there and knew some familiar faces. By then I even understood the lore of Baboon Point which overlooked the bay and could easily evoke the plaintive sounds of both the long-beaked birds and the mining train that made up the audio backdrop to the desert wave.

I even knew other waves nearby, and the contours of the coast; knew where to stay, and how long to stay for. Knew what to pack, and what time the band would be playing in the Hotel Eland that evening; knew how much each mission up there would require – not just in terms of money for petrol, and possible further damage to the ever-fragile Peugeot, but also how to justify it to myself or others. Knew how to rationalise skipping classes or, upsetting others; knew how many times per month I could get away with it (two at the most) and for how long each time (three days and two nights, at a push).

In those days of peak intimacy, now long gone, I had known the rhythm of the place in a way that almost made the wave call out when it was breaking. So, after all that, to come back on a visit after a work trip years later felt somehow offensive to a place with which I had shared so much more than a nodding acquaintance: now, I was on a borrowed board and in a borrowed wetsuit; now, no longer driving in the Peugeot, but a guest in the cars of Matt and others. Now, no longer able quite so much to choose the exact moment of entry and exit from the surf; no longer able to precisely fine tune the Elands experience to capacity and need, mood and desire.

And thus, that day, the wave slipped by: just minutes before, I had deliriously paddled out again after so long away. The water was a deep and dark blue, shimmering in its glassiness. Each individual drop of the breaking curl seemed to be clear and visible in the desert sun; the only problem was to control excitement and enthusiasm and calibrate my advance on the peak: to stop and breathe and relax; to look around and nod, before inching closer to where surfers lay or sat, circling like birds of prey.

Eventually, the chance came. Matt's irate but accurate words from years before still echoed: "Don't even paddle for a wave here, bru, if you aren't going to go." Wise words, undoubtedly, though at times hard to apply: I began to line myself up for a vast long deep blue-black one, breaking fast. The kind of wave that would have set you up for the day, the week, the month.

An Afrikaans surfer, deeply suntanned and with a goatee, was five yards away; I could see he was too far from where the wave would break. He, also, knew he wasn't going to make it, and heroically shouted at me to go. Yet as I turned around quickly, surging with excitement, something was off: it was just that bit too early in the session; I was slightly out of position; the wave was big and breaking fast. Something – maybe the echo of Matt's words, maybe not – held me back.

And so the wave broke, and no one rode it – from the back, the white water rose evenly, like a burning fuse, as it hit the reef and peeled and fizzed down the line. The Afrikaans surfer cried out in anguish: I felt instantly sick with distress and disappointment and knew instantly I would be cursed never to forget that moment. Fortunately, though, the image will always be from seconds before, as the big blue wall bore down on me.

The rest of the session was transcendent, though undistinguished: no more waves like that one came through. Other surfers drifted around, and everyone got some good rides. But maybe that was how it was meant to be: maybe Elands had to be a devotion and an altar, for some at least. Not, I am sure, for visiting pros, or travelling rippers, or Cape Town hellmen – those who could paddle out anywhere, at any time. For others, such as myself, the relationship had to be there for my surfing to work –there had to be a slight (even if imagined) note of communication, empathy, and even the mystical between wave and rider.

Post-Excess at K-Bay
County Dublin, Ireland
Circa 2015

The days of excess, I knew, were ending. As an inadvertent swansong I had engaged in every wild option available notice the night before: what had meant to be a civilised affair for the Barrel Searcher's birthday had unravelled into a night of extremes, culminating in a half-remembered body slam contest on his kitchen table.

In my bleary state, I couldn't determine if the waves that arrived the next day were a curse or a blessing. Were they sent from the heavens to aid recovery; to allow me to lie low, in some form of reclusion, while the worst of the body shocks from the night before passed? As I sat amidst the churning brownish-grey wind swell, feeling cold beneath the light Irish drizzle that is almost (but not quite) rain, it didn't feel that way.

Instead, the tumult of the ocean matched, accentuated, extrapolated internal convulsions and lurches. I felt, for the first time, sea sick as the jumbled waves swam before my eyes. Even clambering to my feet required efforts of will and balance that felt unprecedented in their biomechanical demands; floating beside my board after yet another wipe out, close to vomiting, I made yet another vow to myself to curb such excesses. "Never again," I said to the surfer beside me – famous last words. Yet, as it turned out, this was the vow that worked – at least occasionally – after so many others that had been mere delirium tremens after wild nights.

Riptide at Rockaway
San Mateo, California
Circa November 2016

For quite a few years, Willi and I had had a good groove. For me, freshly back in America and with as yet no wheels, he represented a keen driver and hunter – one who loved nothing more than to scour the coast in his Volvo for offbeat breaks on a Saturday morning, or bunk out of the office on a Tuesday afternoon to surf Ocean Beach when it was good. We worked together at the university, although he was in a far more exalted professional position; thus, to him, I was also an ideal foil: someone to surf with and bounce ideas off, personal and professional.

It was, in some respects, like a surfing golf match, as on each mission the business of African HIV/AIDS programmes was discussed between waves. But it wasn't all just functional: Willi had his own problems in life, his own concerns – despite his suntanned surfer style, despite his unruly curly hair.

In a way then, it evened out: I would discuss relationships and missing home and he, the strains of an overactive mind or an absurdly demanding international travel schedule, in between our mutually flippant remarks on everything else. Overall, though, he of course had the upper hand: on his home turf, and with money and a good job and a settled nature, he could afford to express his occasional concerns with abandon – possibly because mine felt so vast in comparison.

Fuelled with coffee, and constantly changing radio stations with his steering wheel controller in a bid to keep up with his racing, caffeinated thoughts, our conversation would lurch from topic to topic – politics, war, epidemics, earthquakes – as he sped down the coast in the weekend dawn. In my often post-party state, I would regale him with stories of the night before: he was, it seemed, sufficiently amused at tuning into my alternate universe of San Francisco after dark that he was generally ok with sorting the boards as I clambered slowly into my wetsuit. Yet there was no question of inequality on either side: I would pay the price of being a passenger by sometimes having to stay quiet and surf the waves he wanted, and often buying him breakfast to say thanks.

Yet, as with any ostensibly ideal partnership, over time cracks inevitably began to appear. Willi was generally only available when it worked for him and was often away for long periods of travel; eventually, I bought an old pickup truck, which at least meant access to local waves independently.

We both, over time, also forged other surfing relationships. For me, the fellow Irishmen occasionally wanted to go the beach. Willi, also, had other surfing commitments: always extending the invitation to come, just maybe not with such total enthusiasm when conflict arose, there were times when I sensed my presence would not be totally logistically optimal.

And so when, some years into that stage of our groove, I got stuck in the riptide at Rockaway, maybe we both knew it was over. The break is a big right-hander south of San Francisco; off the side of an incline of the Pacific Coast Highway and populated by a local crew. Willi loved it, even lauding the virtues of the wild current that tore along the edge of the cliff and line-up. But I had rarely found waves there and my role that day had yet again drifted into that of spectator. How different to the epic rides I would get at Ocean Beach when choosing wind and tide and conditions myself; he travels fastest who travels alone, I reflected as I felt myself drifting out to sea.

As always, a total gentleman and friend, Willi had already gone in, but from the carpark kept an eye on me as I tried to paddle away from the teeth of the Rockaway rip. It was a big and stormy day, and I knew there were very few options: I didn't want to avail of the nuclear resort of paddling directly into shore and risk getting caught inside by one of the big set waves coming through. If it were to come to that, I knew the change of direction and sprint paddle would have to be timed just right.

And that is the image: of Willi in the car park, and big waves coming through and the sense, undoubtedly, that enough was enough. That our chemical reaction was no longer working so well, despite the previously-benign combination of our styles, and that we both knew it – that this might be our last surf trip together, at least for a while.

In a more benign interpretation, I knew also that we had both, maybe, reached better stages: Willi now having overcome academic edginess to establish himself as a stylish surfer, an old salt, and a charger; I having earned and learned enough independence to surf solo in the USA. Even our talks on epidemiology had had their day; with nothing said, and no bad vibes, we moved from one stage of camaraderie to the next.

What followed would, in academic terms, be called an emeritus relationship: occasional offers of surf trips still appear from both sides, and there will always be the dubious bond of too many cold and grey San Francisco dawn patrols endured together.

View from the hill in Santa Cruz; setting up at Bruce's; considering next life moves over a Tecate on Wilbur Street.

Soul Time

Small day at the Slab (Frog Rock).

Even at the best of times, there are gaps. Even when everything is groovy, life throws up lulls and transitions and limbos, days or weeks or even months of uncertainty. Times of being on call, or on yellow alert, or of not knowing what the future holds; of waiting for exam results or job offers; times when there is nothing to do but sit on your hands, or bite your knuckles. Times when one dreams of something – anything – to alleviate pressures of waiting or fear; times when any alternative to running over past and future possibilities is a welcome respite.

Nature abhors a vacuum, and there are times when even the antics of wave-riding won't fill the gap. Yet there are moments, also, when surfing becomes a secret power: moments of disappearing down the beach and paddling out in to flat or bad surf, if for no other reason than to return to land having experienced something new.

That is not to say that surfing is always a cure for spiritual angst: in many cases the disappointment of uneventful beach time only numbs or dazes. Sometimes nothing happens in a session, good or bad: but, generally, there is at least something to be reviewed and discussed and troubleshot over the hours to come; something to be slept on, or discussed with a mate, until new conclusions emerge.

This, amidst all that, is the soul of surfing: the times when there is nothing to do but chill out and sit or lie on your board and check out the horizon, the sky. That is not to say that there is necessarily any kind of spiritual side in operation, any more than there is to bike riding or mountain walking: surfing, unlike yoga or other quasi-mystical pursuits, lays no claim to communion with higher powers and inner peace. But, like anything, it can sometimes offer windows onto the soul.

Windows from moments: between sets, or out the back. From gazing at the sun or horizon or ocean surface or sky: time to let bad news sink in, or process good tidings, or brace for future gnarliness or positive change. A time to put events into perspective – maybe on occasion glancing upwards, wondering and gesturing, like a footballer coming on to the pitch.

These are the times that spiritual leaders appreciate and record in other settings but are baffled by in surfing: maybe because it takes place so far from shore, there is no immediate or tangible karmic or behavioural dividend. Surfing offers us few examples of shoplifters who can be pointed to as having stopped stealing; few precedents of criminals who achieved redemption in the same way as having joined the YMCA or the church. Wave-riding, without such formal structures and taking place out to sea, changes vibes in perhaps less visible ways.

Life doesn't necessarily switch direction after such surf-spirit experiences – they are not magically transformative. But, sometimes, they can be the start of something different – can jog one out of old routines or habits with alarming abruptness; can change perspectives on self and status or on plans, disappointments, and the outside world. Likewise, the sea can demand reassessments of priorities, or act as the catalyst for a domino effect (to mix metaphors) like a stone thrown into a lake: those are the moments when surfing is at its most soulful, and it has little to do with tube riding or staying in the curl. When a glimpse of alternative universes is offered, just when the *status quo* is wearing you down, nature is pleased: the vacuum has, even if only briefly, been filled.

Skunked
Anywhere
Anytime

Sometimes desperation for waves, combined with absurd optimism, trumps common sense. On such days, surfers need the capacity to deceive themselves – Shakespearian suspension of disbelief. A capacity to ignore facts and figures, common sense and wind direction – but overriding intuition is always an edgy vibe, and always, somewhere in the subconscious, one feels doomed from the start.

Thus the feeling of arriving to no surf has no real up sides, maybe, except the sense of subconscious triumph: there can be disappointment, dejection, disgust – except, of course, somewhere inside, you knew this was going to happen. Yet even after years of experience – even after multiple such Groundhog Days – the dream of catching an improbable wave or two can deceive even the most level head.

The beginning of the skunk is usually the view, but it can also be the quiet: the unique silence that accompanies a lack of breaking waves. At the end of a walk to shore, the waves – or where the waves should be – come into field of vision. The walk itself has probably been rushed and hassled, with an edge of urgency: a need to get the bad news over with; a hunger and yearning to be proved wrong; a faint hope that there might be something there.

That is, maybe, followed by parking lot or roadside or clifftop disbelief or denial – where are the waves? Are they hiding; is this a lull in the sets? Is the swell due to arrive within the hour; is swell direction changing the arrival point; are there any hints or clues that might suggest that something rideable might appear – or, worse, that it has just disappeared? In the latter case, such circumstances have been immortalised in some of the most painful words a surfer can ever hear: "You should have been here yesterday."

While desperately straining eyes to see if there is anything makeable on the crumbling shore, break reality simultaneously sets in: Plan Bs are initiated. Would the best choice, maybe, be to cut and run: to pretend the mission had never happened, and hasten homewards? Damage limitation can cause its own damage, however: there are days when there is no choice but to suit up and paddle out – to stay and pray, if for no other reason than to wash off the drive down.

Even then, a sense of the ridiculous persists: to the casual observer, a wet-suited surfer on a board on a flat sea looks ridiculous, delusional. "But these are no waves," they say to you – as if you didn't know. It is hardly worth explaining that the effort is now just for exercise, for sun, or maybe the odd encounter with a seal or porpoise or dolphin: hard to explain that the whole production has turned into soul time, and a salvage operation.

Yes, skunked – the only inadequate word for such an inadequate experience. Yet somehow, if you can be motivated to get in the water at all, you feel better coming out – as if some kind of karmic deal has been made, and the surf will more likely be up the next time you drive down. And, more than that, to have been out there chilling out – away from the frenzy of good waves; to have been on a beach bereft of surfers, drifting in the water, out of hunt mode – sometimes has its own benefits. The soul time: that your subconscious will eventually tell you, was the whole point – the real need that had to be fulfilled.

K-Bay Shorebreak
County Dublin, Ireland
November 1996

The cross-country missions were, it appeared, only one part of the surfing hazing that would be required for the Emerald Isle. What really mattered was how you managed the K-Bay shore break. That, I was told by old hands, was what counted.

Still buoyed from Californian successes, I reckoned I was ready for a bigger winter day at what we called (in ironic homage to the South African abbreviation for Jeffrey's Bay) K-Bay. But, to make matters more complex, it was a break across from the house I had grown up in, and one that – if surfing was or wasn't to work out – would haunt me for ever if I failed. Not until having the measure of that wave could I ever again feel comfortable at home; I reckoned I would, otherwise, evermore feel I was hiding from it when it appeared.

The day I took it on was both the start and the end of something: the abrupt end to newfound California perceptions of surfing and the world as sunny, gentle places and groovy experiences without harsh sides; as frictionlessly smooth. As I bounced down the cold steps to the stony beach with bleached blond hair (and the equally sun-bleached Cruiser under my arm), fresh from sunlit beaches, I still held on to those dreamy notions.

But it was also the start of something else: a new phase was about to begin. As I paddled out in a lull, the haze of the party the night before was quickly washed away by cold Irish Sea water. The ocean, that day, had an energy to it (though I wasn't to know it at the time) that I was to later associate with bigger surf – the waves themselves felt more alive, more visceral. Finding a gap in the sets with typical beginner's luck, I threaded out towards the ominously-titled group of K-Bay Hellmen – a pack of local, good old boys – to smile and nod and talk about how cool it all was.

All of that – a whole era of life, a whole set of perceptions – ended with stomach-lurching suddenness when the board I was sitting on rose abruptly, like an elevator. I had been lifted by a set wave line of swell passing underneath me, and – even though I had been prepared – its size had lurched my stomach in the same way as skateboarding down a hill too fast. It was a roller coaster, speed-wobble sensation, which let me know immediately and unquestionably that I was, in every sense of the word, out of my depth.

With my tail already between my legs, it seemed pointless to hang around: morale had slipped irrecoverably, and there was already no hope of redemption that day. Who knew if I would surf there again – who cared, as long as I got back to the beach, and out of a zone that could only now bring fear and embarrassment: behind the sympathetic glances of the pack, I was, in my distress, sure that there was an element of newbie-flash-in-the-pan dismissiveness as well.

Paddling back towards the beach, the two standout surfers – OMA and the Tinker – had told me as I passed to time it right; to watch for gaps in the sets that would let me get to shore relatively unmolested. But, by that stage of the afternoon the wind was rising and added to the roar of the waves, their "no, no, no" turned, in my ears, to "go, go, go."

And so, exiting stage left, I paddled as hard as I could towards the beach. I was there: I could see the gleam of the wet and rounded stones on the shore, each mirroring the grey sky in one quadrant. I was, at that moment, maybe six feet from land, and two feet above sea level.

So near, yet so far. Another novel sensation was to arise abruptly that day: the unearthly feeling of being pulled far back from the shore, and far above it, at the very second it looked close. The numbers were flipped, as I realised I was now just two feet from the stones and rocks – but six feet above them: the infamous K-Bay shorebreak, in which dying waves break abruptly on the beach, had me in its teeth.

But no time to think: only a fraction of a second to see the stones glimmer, and marvel at the bizarreness of the situation; only time to bid a last farewell to California clichés, and hope for the best. No time, except to catch a glimpse of the rocks beneath framed in the gutturally sucking grey water as the wave paused for a second and, having collected me, dropped me off.

As most surfers do (and possibly explaining their occasional spiritual side) I escaped unharmed – merely drilled sideways into the beach, and pulled back again, and drilled twice more before scrambling away. Careless of my beautiful board, the only choice was to eventually struggle to my feet and humiliatingly drag it behind me by the leash, praying that it didn't suck me back into the maw. (Later, peeling off my wetsuit, a clattering sound brought curious gazes. Somehow, the force of the water had lodged a vast amount of small stones between my skin and the wetsuit; I hadn't felt them come in.)

At least, I supposed, something had happened. There had been amusement and entertainment, provided gratis by ambition, delusion, and over-optimism: two of the Hellmen, OMA and the Tinker, said they would never forget the sight. But maybe more importantly, something – anything – had happened, on a wintery Irish day. Something that wasn't domestic, or academic, or related to work, or the day-to-day: something, however bizarre, for the soul.

Got a Little Over-Excited
Sydney, Australia
Circa April 2000

Not a dark and stormy night, but a cold and grey Sydney morning, with a new swell: a building swell, evolving from the evenly spaced lines of surf of the night before. And a cold swell – gun metal grey on a weekday dawn, with not many others out. Just a few of the faces that had by now become familiar: the less razzle dazzle characters; the ones who were always there, even when it was cold. One of them was a wiry man who was half bald, surfed well, and gave me the occasional nod. And all of us, to suit the setting, were clad in jet black wetsuits.

For once, one of the reefer-addled surfers with whom I was living in Australia with had come down as well. As a result, the stakes felt quite high: even though there was no peanut gallery (with few on the beach, and no one on Bondi's Campbell Parade looking all that interested) some upper-echelon locals were there, and a mate as well. Unfortunately, as other distractions had clouded the capacity of many to get to the beach, I had become used to surfing alone and anonymously – which were now (surprisingly) the conditions under which when I surfed best. No eyes or pressures, distractions or Kodak courage: just waves and paddle and positioning, take-off and ride.

And the surf was getting better before our eyes. It was still a full tide; the sets were still breaking just close enough to the beach to give it a kind of grandstand feel. The swell was also coming at an angle, producing lefts that looked like perfect point break waves: funnelling and racing down the beach, they were not over-fast or over-hollow breach break barrels, for once, but instead benign and beautiful to behold. And thus in surprise – even though there weren't many other surfers to manoeuvre with – I found myself in the right spot on what was to us the first wave of the day.

Drifting up to what had become the outer point, a dark blue wave came through: around four to six feet high and peeling along the shore. I span around to go for it, and instantly felt the sets of eyes watching me. It didn't matter: though I didn't usually like surfing in the morning as much as the mellow and golden Australian evenings, this was all just so right. The right board, right spot, and no one else paddling for it: a headline moment, so early in the day.

Yet somehow, I missed it, blew it, felt the wave take me, got to my feet, and spectacularly overbalanced on the bottom turn. There was no reason why; just one of those things. Nineteen times out of twenty, maybe, I would have nailed it, and lapsed straight into that magical surf rhythm that lets you keep nailing it, wave after wave, over and over, for hours at a time.

I made quite a splash, so maybe the moment at least looked entertaining in its tragedy. There were other waves in the set, but the event had caught the attention of the surfers: there had been, I knew, an almost audible cringe when I blew it. My fellow Irishman looked fixedly at the horizon, trying not to laugh as he sat on his board. Only the Aussie, whose respect I valued equally, looked over at me with a raised eyebrow. "Got a little overexcited, eh?" Somehow, it didn't feel bad, the way he said it.

The Drive to Byron
New South Wales, Australia
May 2000

By the time we reached Lennox, the wheels were falling off. Not literally: the rental car that had ferried el Senor, the Masochist and I up the coast from Sydney towards the then-mythical environs of

Byron Bay had held out. Less so, temperaments: the after-effects of wild nights, overtiredness, and fraternal rivalries had started to override the country feeling vibe we had sought.

The mission had begun well enough: Senor, flying in tornado-fashion from London for a two-week surf break midway through a year in Australia for the younger crew, had engineered a trip up the coast. That in itself was no bad thing: the predominance of a nocturnal lifestyle had taken its toll on many, leaving lassitude and edginess in its wake. Though no kind of purist, surfing at Bondi had for me been an escape from many of the worst temptations; others had no such outlets, and there was an urgent need for a breath of – quite literally – fresh air.

Yet we weren't quite out of the woods: I had tried to play my cards right, as the only non-brother aboard, but also knew both of them well enough that they would eventually reach breaking point. Shamefully, that didn't bother me: at least there was the certain knowledge I would never be *persona non grata*; that they would each be looking for backup in scoring a point against the other or, seeking a casting vote. Thus protected, I tried to avoid taking sides, and sat back to enjoy the ride.

The meltdown, when it came, arrived from an unforeseen angle: not debate over destination or who had to do the next spell of driving; not choice of surf spot, or hunger, or needing to stop to take a piss. The crux, instead, was the rental car air conditioning: did it run off the battery, or petrol? If the latter, as one bro insisted, we had better turn it off on order to conserve rations until we reached the next town. If the former – as the other brother claimed, as if his life depended on it – we should press on with the cool air on full blast in the sultry Australian night. After all, we had waves to catch.

The debate simmered, then raged: in the pre-internet and smart phone age, there was no easy way of proving right or wrong. Both sides dug their heels in; I can't remember the outcome, and to this day still don't know the answer. But – whatever it was – by the time we reached Byron, antagonism and hurt feelings had descended so deeply that even the protectiveness of neutrality had lost its allure. Reach-around car seat punches had been attempted, voices had been raised, threats made; precedent-skeletons dug up, along the endless stream of cats' eyes and double-yellow-line road divider that would continue up the coast.

Long-term damage to relationships threatened, but resolution came in an equally unexpected way: the next morning, the debate still burning, we cruised along Byron's slightly Wild West main street. There, in a surf shop, el Senor was engaged unexpectedly in conversation by a gnarled-looking biker: amidst tattoos and leather jackets and aircon discussion, gradually and tentatively the conversation turned to surfboards. Thus el Senor cruised into the surf shop, and began to examine surf craft – querying technicalities, and describing to the biker his failure to find the right board for him so eloquently that it became release – a surf-talk therapy session, maybe.

The Masochist, now chilled out though his own means, strolled over after the soliloquy. El Senor, looking round as if awakened from a dream, decided that the place was cool – that he would cruise around a bit, and meet up with us later. Over the coming days we surfed sublime topical waves, Aircongate now a thing of the past.

The Bus to Ocean Beach
San Francisco, California
Circa March 2003

It was triumph, it was humiliation. But, taking the bus to the beach in San Francisco in the days before I had a car was mainly just convenient – I could take the Five Fulton or the Twenty-One Hayes from my apartment and be dropped, twenty minutes later, at the northern end of Ocean Beach near the Wise Surf Shop. Those were days when buses felt easy and relaxed – when the city wasn't quite so efficient, quite so techy and crowded, as it is now. Often, there would be empty rides on old machines, giving one time to read or stare out the window and take America in.

But when I began to bring a surfboard and wetsuit with me, the stakes rose somewhat. In those days, almost anything went in

San Francisco, and a surfboard was just another variation on a piercing or tattoo (if a little harder to transport). Very occasionally, drivers would say no, or ask you to wait for the next one if the bus was crowded, but that was fair enough: half-expected setbacks, nothing to spoil the day.

What was harder, maybe, was within: the challenges of sitting on a bus with a surfboard in the land of the automobile. In the days before the mainstreaming of surfboard bike carriers or beachside equipment lockers, it seemed to be the only way to get equipment to the surf without wheels. That, in turn, was part of my broader strategy at the time: of trying to hold back on big investments such as cars and couches until I understood San Francisco and its pitfalls slightly better.

But there was a price to be paid: bringing surfboards on Californian public transport is an art form that quickly loses its allure, and once past a certain age is robbed even of the youthful and naïve backpacker aesthetic. Behind my board bag, I would try to make myself as discreet and invisible as possible, to avoid bewildered stares or *sotto voce* complaints.

But the bus was only the first stage of vulnerability, of high stakes: there then had to be negotiated in the surf shop or the Beach Chalet (a local down-home restaurant) where, in those easy-going days, if you found the right person they would let you store your gear with only a mildly bewildered look. Even that was worth tolerating for the luxury of not having to leave clothes and keys on the beach: no craning my neck between sets to double check that everything was still there, though no rogue hippy or tweaker ever touched them. Some even had a hose and faucet to rinse off with, if one asked nicely.

Yet none of it was ever encouraged; there was a vague sense of trespass throughout, and it never became an easy routine in the way I had felt it in Southern California or Portugal: the flip flop style I was trying to pull off in chilly and foggy San Francisco had not, it seemed, often been attempted before. But, despite all of that, there was a simplicity, a reductionism, and a good vibe to it all.

The surfs themselves were rarely memorable, but good things happened: days of meeting other surfers for the first time or earned some begrudging respect from the surf shop staff, both groups bemused at my dedication to the beach. Days, also, when the coast felt it has been opened up and San Francisco no longer seemed as much of an urban jungle; days of energy and independence and freedom; days when there was time and space to reflect and recover from the night before.

But even after the surf, the trials were not over: changing (worst in the rain), retrieving gear, and negotiating the bus home all had to be addressed. There were no offers of a place to store a board at the shop, so the bus diver on the way back had little choice but to take you or to make you walk. Finally, back to the apartment and a night out in town and a surf story to tell: mission accomplished and, likely to be attempted again the next day.

Maybe I am wrong, but in 2020 I am pretty sure those days have gone. I am not on the bus to the beach that much anymore, though, so it is impossible to say. But one senses that, with the new rules and regulations that are added to our lives each day, some kind of policy regarding surfboards – most likely now classified as oversize luggage – is now in place. To be honest, I wouldn't want to have to try to find out.

Bruce's
Eastern Cape, South Africa
May 2005

After a week at a place called Seal Point, even the most spiritualised, surf drenched South African trip – even with the best *braais* and the best conditions, even with clean water and warm waves – needs an adjustment. Not much, though: maybe just a trip around the corner to Jeffrey's Bay, just for a change. Anything, really, that takes away the perfection of Seals just to bring it back again in enhanced form. Even just a walk on the wild side (literally), along the rocks east of Cape Saint Francis and past the lighthouse, was sometimes enough. There, winding trails ran along the shore, and very occasional old-school cottages dotted the route.

But that was Seals and the Full Stop Rock (and the Full Stop Pub) and a different story, one that has been told by others many times. This one is about a wave called Bruce's Beauties: about waking up one morning, peering out of the surf trip tent, and seeing swell in the water that was missing the bay. Well, if not quite missing it, then at least not quite hitting it right: the quasi-mystical Bruce's that breaks only when every star aligns might be working, I half-dreamed, clambering out of the tent flap.

There was no real reason why I should have thought it would work. For sure, I had done my share of reading and amateur oceanography, but this was different: just a hunch, when I saw the way the ocean looked. Just one of those occasions that comes up very, very rarely, and mainly for those with plenty of time on their hands: moments for those who had the capacity to wait for days and weeks for something right to happen, and to be on it when it did. Waking a sleeping lass, we drove our ancient Peugeot the short distance up to Saint Francis Bay in the dawn; after a little nosing around, we found the break.

I had been wrong. There were lines of swell, but it wasn't breaking. Or maybe it was, but it didn't really look like it: at best, it was a miniature version of the cinematic *Endless Summer* dream; equally far removed from the big and hollow waves that one associates with modern Bruce's. Still, it was a very sunny and very quiet morning; no one was out, and we were there now. Knowing my partner in crime would be distressed at our dawn patrol if it didn't pay some kind of dividend, I got in.

The rest is a surf fairy story: paddling out, I could see the waves looked better from sea level rather than from the slightly elevated bluff over the rocks we had been watching from. Even better, whatever Bruce's wanted in terms of tide and swell and direction and wind was happening: the sets started to improve. The water (maybe it was just the time of day) was ultra-green and clear; I was solo, but there was no sense of sharkiness.

I caught a lot of waves that day, the board skipping gently over the slight texture in the face each time, so the moment wasn't about a single ride: surfed for many hours; came in and paddled out again more than once. On one such occasion, there was a bewildered South African lady on an early cell phone. "It's breaking," I overheard her saying in excitement. "No, bizarre, nobody out – just this one ou."[*]

The wave itself, I was slowly realising as what I was experiencing sank in, was almost a work of art. The take-offs were easy, like a friendly point wave – like as the inside of J-Bay. But then – over and over – there followed the unique green walls and little cover up sections for maybe twenty or thirty yards, maybe more. The waves had that reeling quality that is a sign of a truly great surfing set-up; there was something preternaturally consistent about their shape; about the way they broke over the big, rounded boulders that lined the shore. Something, maybe, to do with the curve of the face and curl that suggested ease and predictability: something that told you that the wave was so good, it would do all the work for you.

There – riding in the pocket under the curl on a mythical wave in warm water on a sunny day – something else might have happened; the day at Bruce's had another angle as well. For quite a long time in South Africa, I had been searching for something that might distinguish my two years there from the experience a surf tourist who merely timed swells right might have had: at Bruce's, maybe, there was that distinction and that rarity. In turn, it meant that so much else had come together: that my confidence, initially eroded by Africa, was returning; that my life judgement in choosing to live there for a while had not been totally off.

But to get Bruce's like that – to be in the right place, at the right time – was above all down to luck. Sure, there was also an element of strategy and style that played a part – an element of finally having my act together. It was a time of finally winning battles with the mechanics of the Peugeot's engine; of calm in a tempestuous relationship; of when the mere fact of being in South

---

[*] Afrikaans slang for person, human, or surfer.

Africa all came together: finally, the investment of time and life in surfing were all now, finally, worth it. The radical hazing of life in Africa had ended there at Bruce's even though it never does; my efforts to get the right board shaped by Pierre, and to learn coastlines and conditions and cultures, had finally paid off.

It was one of those benign spells in the middle of a stage of life, maybe, when everything had been trialled and errored: a time when there was no debating about which wetsuit to use (a slightly worn four-three) or whether to wear booties (no) or which board to use (a seven-two, out of respect to Bruce's, as much as out of not wanting to miss a wave there): an all-too-brief existential sweet spot.

The day was, to most, nothing epic or unforgettable – otherwise, the crowds would surely have been on it. But, for the travelling solo surfer, it was the coolest of scenarios: an anonymous Tuesday morning in May, or whenever it was, when most civilised people were in offices or with families. When most were doing school runs, or shopping, or working, or studying, or painting and decorating, or whatever – doing, basically, useful and meaningful things – Bruce's had given the day some kind of direction as well.

Lissadell with Brucey and American Guest
County Sligo, Ireland
January 2014

The surfboards had lain between us all the way around Ireland. From the Blarney Stone to the Cliffs of Moher – through Kinvara, and via Renvyle House – the visiting Hawaiian-American lady had gazed at them from the passenger seat of my borrowed Mum's car, rather than gaze at me. It had been an accident of design, though not necessarily a malign one: there was, at least no danger of my taking my eyes off the treacherously winding Irish coastal roads to look meaningfully into hers; no danger, either, of boredom at the sight of each other. Instead, at the end of each leg, she was a pleasantly original vision – maybe I was as well, though that was never confirmed.

But as with any surf trip – particularly the ones that attempt to combine charm and tourism, drinking and dancing, and an element of romance – there had been strain. Eventually, subtly, the presence of the surfboards was called into question: "Were they even going to be used?" she wondered aloud, or had I merely brought them to avoid looking at her? Thus checkmated, without now finding waves the entire paradigm – the smartness and style and spirit of the trip – would be called into question. Surfing had gone from an option to an imperative; without waves, the boards would only ever be looked upon as a divisive physical barrier.

Eventually, going from hotels to hostels and back again, we wound our way to Donegal and Bundoran – erstwhile home of Brucey, an overworked doctor and occasional party boy (later to become a monk). In between his ever-more–frequent meditation retreats, he still had time for an old mate: we ate cheap Indian food in town and told stories of the old days. The price of road trips can be high one for everyone; to be able to jive with one of the good old boys was quite possibly even more welcome to her than it was to me.

And yet, the feel of the trip remained shaky. Brucey, progressing further and further down the path of spiritualism and bachelorhood, had a spare room that was fittingly scented more with old wetsuits than *eau de cologne.* Having just returned from a series of missions to far-out parts of Africa and the Middle East, which had often required aromatic digs, the hotel we explored as an alternative offered little solace either: eventually, after a private and protracted assessment of the challenges of each, we gratefully settled back *chez Bruce* and resigned ourselves to the salty, musty ambience.

The next day, the town dawned grey and still: for an urbane American visitor, there was the distinct possibility that an off-season Irish coastal locale might fail to appeal. Bundoran, rather than having the charms of a rural harbour village or a whitewashed cottage motif, instead had very little to entice in the off-season if you weren't into pubs, takeaways and amusement arcades.

So, expecting little, we drove south just for something to do. The surfboard had to be used somehow, and Bundoran's world-class waves weren't delivering: we wound, instead, down country lanes, past W.B. Yeats' grave and to a country-soul peak called Lissadell, where – at last – the swell was arriving. Bidding a brief *adieu* to my patient companion, Brucey and I paddled out to hook a few.

Looking back to shore, she could be seen gazing out: with her characteristic impassivity now swaddled in layers of scarves, it was impossible to tell if she was enjoying herself or not. To some, if not to many, it might be a welcome situation: green rolling hills on a peaceful stretch of Irish coast, surrounded by somnolent noise of surf and sheep and cows. But, to others, it might seem a hell hole, far from the comforts of civilisation: with visitors to Ireland, I had found you could never really tell if they were enjoying themselves or not. Maybe, sometimes, they weren't even sure themselves.

Eventually, paddling in, I peered into her eyes for a clue as to satisfaction or admiration, despair or chagrin. But there was nothing: no way to tell if the surf had been a welcome diversion or a footnote to a trip around a country that invariably challenged as many visitors as it charmed. But, if nothing else, at least the boards had been used – at least it had been proven that they weren't there merely as prop, or distraction. She had seen, she said neutrally as we changed, Brucey and I catching waves on the inside – even though her eyes weren't up to distinguishing one black-clad figure from another.

On the way, home, finally, she broke another long polite silence: she was glad, she said, that the boards had been used. Glad to have seen people catch waves in Ireland, possibly us, and had been pleased to meet Brucey; glad I had some good old boys. But none of that compared to the combined astonishment and fear she then said she had felt when as she watched the black dots floating far from shore: for people to sit above water that deep, she said, was beyond her comprehension. Weren't we afraid of drowning? That, and that alone, was the bizarre feature that had inadvertently impressed her, and possibly made the surf worthwhile.

Ocean Beach Dolphins
San Francisco, California
Circa 2017

The man in the surf shop had told me that there had never been a shark attack there: despite its position within the Californian red triangle of the Farallon Islands, Stinson Beach and Santa Cruz – bisecting one of its daunting sides – Ocean Beach repelled sharks. Local lore said it was because it was too close to the mouth of San Francisco Bay, or that the titanium grains of sand of the beach were too fine and minute for the sharks' tastes: with their propensity to cloud the water, they had clearer and cleaner places to be. But not so the dolphins.

There was a time when dolphin experiences were memorable – worth writing home about. Times when they felt transcendent and electric; times when they alone would be enough for fulfilment and thrill. Yet over the years, and with a hundred exposures, the wild surges of excitement had started to fade with familiarity. The coolest and most experienced surfers at Ocean Beach never turned a hair (or even an eye) as pods rolled meanderingly past, sliding up and out of the water, looking at you out of the corner of their eyes. Still, each time there was a sense of reassurance and *joie de vivre* and thrill that was irrepressible: the closer they got, the stronger all of that was.

As a result, even after a hundred encounters the dolphins still had the capacity to imprint on memory. There was still the surge of interest as a pod came towards one, noisily: spitting spray carelessly in the air, and slipping by with an otherwise silent oily sheen below the water. Yet they are big (sometimes eight or ten feet long) and wild animals, so there never total tranquillity – it is on a ponderous collision course; has it seen you? Is he or she in maybe a bad mood, or protecting its young? Or has it just finally had enough of the men in wetsuits dangling their legs into its element, as they sit in majestic trespass on their boards?

If they have any such qualms, they haven't yet shown them – haven't yet displayed irritation or bad vibes or annoyance, at least not to me. Instead, they have brought only reassurance – when you see dolphins, surf speak goes, you are never going to see a shark – and occasional mind-blowing visuals when, on certain rare days, they surf in the waves, or exuberantly flip out of the ocean to flap fins before plunging back beneath.

During an era when I was often in the ocean on off days and bad days – on grey days and small days; on windy days, or when the tide was wrong – I met a lot of dolphins. On dog days, with no one else out, often the only way to pass the time (apart from paddling from peak to peak, lateral to the shore, in a vague attempt at exercise) was to either watch the pelicans surf lines of swell, or wait for the dolphins.

On just such a day, with only a few other surfers dotted around, I was sitting out the back as a dolphin some distance out to sea flipped and jumped. As it came towards shore, it closed in on me, its jumps marking its trajectory: a flip and a wag and a disappearance, before repeating the same unusual pattern. On its last flight, judging its intervals, I half-expected it to hit my board. Instead, it leapt into the sky just yards away – a moment frozen in time – and dived again, beneath my feet and under the board, before surfacing for another flourish on the other side.

The moment was so sudden that there was no time to react – time only to lodge the image of its rise and fall on either side, and to feel momentarily its power and strength. The plunge was audible – I was hit by the splash. The dolphin, surely, had been playing with me – nothing malicious or malign, just some fun and games, some cat-and-mouse, as it went on to wherever it was going.

Nearby, a stranger sitting on a surfboard hooted and shouted. He was stoked to have seen what happened, he said, and told me that it looked as if the dolphin was about to hit me; said he had never seen one come that close.

We exchanged a few other Californian words on how groovy dolphins were, and then drifted apart. The dolphin was gone, the other surfer was gone: after a wildly transcendent moment, everything was abruptly quiet again. No one else was around, no one else had seen what happened – nature had left no trace, except for the memory of the shiny grey body, the droplets of water, and the sound of the impact.

Redemption at Ocean Beach
San Francisco, California
October 2018

After a long recovery from a burst appendix, Ocean Beach, on return, seemed both the same and intimidatingly strange. It wasn't the beach that had changed – the easy familiarity required for such a moody place can only be gained after at least a few sessions. (Usually, the first surf there after a long absence is characterised by disaster and missed timing verging on incompetence, as your body begins to remember what to do: the counterpoise to such demoralisation is that the second surf is often very, very good.) No it wasn't the beach – it was something else.

This time, the refamiliarising cycle compressed itself: multiple aspects of micro-evolution seemed to combine to occur at once. At times, it felt like an entire surfing life telescoped into a single session: first, the trepidation and fear of the beginner, as an unsmiling and eagle-nosed surfer cruised past, his hood revealing only a stony and glaring circle of visage. So soon after getting in, the overriding feeling was of inexplicable inadequacy and out-of-place-ness – a childhood sensation. Steering clear of him, I drifted further down the beach.

Still settling my nerves into my newly-vulnerable state – there had been only swashbuckling confidence on the beach – another unknown surfer called me over. Blithely curious, he asked about the somewhat bizarre board I was riding and paddled over for a closer look. Explaining that the Green Bean was an experiment, while also not wanting to take my eyes off the horizon for too long, his good vibes had made a difference: some internal system had been reset, and there it was: instantly, the capacity to catch waves again. In comparative life-cycle terms, the edge and brittle confidence of adolescence – of new mates in a new school, maybe – had been attained.

The wave came, with the friendly surfer in full view on the shoulder as I surfed. He gave a smile and a hoot, examining not so much me but the way the board glided over the water: it was a medium size right-hander, offering only a few seconds of open face before forcing a fast exit over the back. But it had been enough: the floodgates of confidence and belief had been opened. The passage from abject beginner to able-bodied surfer had happened in the space of just a few minutes; I had gone from timid youth to feeling my oats in the metaphorical equivalent.

Then – after a slack spell, when potentialities revealed themselves, and when the joy of surf took hold again – came the time of plenty: it was time to reap the harvest of waves from the surf fields of OB. Like an exuberant animal, over the next hour I felt the resources and capacity and fitness – the will and hunger and desire – all together: in a blur, wave after wave was added to my tally. Similarly, my mindset changed from explorer to hunter, patrolling the line-up like a bird of prey and into position for the next set.

Soon after came exhaustion– slowing down; letting waves go under my feet; tired from the proverbial looting. As with life, I reflected, maybe if there had been a little bit more restraint during the surfeit, I would still have been in action, but it all evened out – who knows, the swell might have faded, or wind changed, had I waited. Better to make hay while the sun shines: I was content now to watch others take off and pick off the occasional one that came along. At one point, the dolphins appeared on their evening cruise down the beach: it was enough just to watch them slide by.

And then the finale – paddling in, as night fell. Tired – overtired – but, for better or for worse, never giving up: picking waves off, or trying to, until it was impossible to distinguish their shape. Until it was too dark to see: washed ashore in the dusk, stoked, and all played out. So much of life's twists and turns had been represented, to a possibly overactive imagination, by an otherwise-innocuous first surf back.

Moments to reflect: J-Bay; E-Bay; K-Bay.

Afterword

"Hawaii '85"
Malibu, California
Summer 1997

McLainer, having deemed us ready – in the realms not just of ability but also etiquette, culture, and fitness – had ferried us the however-many-hours north from Mission Beach to the surfing epicentre of Malibu. There, we had traded waves amidst the crowds and with Miki Dora and Gidget in mind.

Jimmy Snukka and I sat on the beach afterwards, back, as at the beginning, amidst the mellow beach vibe of Southern California. Ahead of us, a gangly, bearded, and old-looking gentleman began to engage in a series of unusual poses before paddling out: yoga wasn't as mainstream in 1997 as it is now, so we watched with interest. And we weren't the only ones checking him out: a fellow old-school surfer strolled up to him, asking if he was who he thought he was. As it turned out, he was: the two exchanged greetings, asking when they last saw each other: "Hawaii, '85, right?" "Right on...." "Been a long time...."

Later, enquires revealed the bearded one as John Peck, pioneer of Malibu and surfer to the bone. But his identity maybe wasn't as important as his vibe: in that moment, the lasting nature of surfing relations was exemplified. To him and his buddy, time didn't really matter that much: one went where the currents of life dictated and sooner or later, you might wash up side by side again.

That, maybe, is the whole point: surfing, and its friendships, bends the rules of time. Whether it is a dozen days or a dozen years since you last saw your protagonist, threads can be picked up as if it was yesterday: that drop-in still rankles; that image of his or her ride is still imprinted on memory; he or she still owes you a beer – all that kind of thing. So, in a way, maybe surfing recall in memory doesn't matter that much: in the end, as that

Frenchman said, though many things change, a whole lot also stays the same…

Printed in Great Britain
by Amazon

83210083R00144